Program Planning and Evaluation for Blind and Visually Impaired Students

National Guidelines for Educational Excellence

Jack Hazekamp and Kathleen Mary Huebner, editors

American Foundation for the Blind, New York

Program Planning and Evaluation for Blind and Visually Impaired Students:
National Guidelines for Educational Excellence
is copyright ©1989 by

American Foundation for the Blind
15 West 16th Street
New York, NY 10011

The American Foundation for the Blind (AFB) is a national nonprofit organization that advocates, develops, and provides programs and services to help blind and visually impaired people achieve independence with dignity in all sectors of society.

Chapters 1–6, appendixes B and D, and portions of appendixes A and G and the glossary have been edited and reprinted with permission of the California State Department of Education from *Program Guidelines for Visually Impaired Individuals,* which was published by the California State Department of Education, 721 Capitol Mall, Sacramento, California (mailing address: P.O. Box 944272, Sacramento, CA 94244-2720), printed by the Office of State Printing, and distributed under the provisions of the Library Distribution Act and *Government Code* Section 11096. Copies of *Program Guidelines for Visually Impaired Individuals* are available for $6 per copy, plus sales tax for California residents, from Publications Sales, California State Department of Education, P.O. Box 271, Sacramento, CA 95802-0271. For information on brailled copies, please contact Multiple Services Media Technology, Inc. (MSMT), 1186 Yulupa Ave., Suite 349, Santa Rosa, CA 95405, (707) 586-1999.
©Copyright, California State Department of Education, 1986, 1987.

Printed in the United States of America

Library of Congress Cataloging-in-Publication Data

Program planning and evaluation for blind and visually
    impaired students.

    Bibliography: p.
    1. Children, Blind--Education--United States.
2. Visually handicapped children--Education--United
States. I. Hazekamp, Jack. II. Huebner, Kathleen
Mary. III. American Foundation for the Blind.
HV1793.P76 1989   371.91'1'0973   89-6970
ISBN 0-89128-155-X

To THE LATE JOSEPHINE L. TAYLOR, a national leader in the education of blind and visually impaired children and youths. Dr. Taylor was involved from the earliest stages in the development of California's *Program Guidelines for Visually Impaired Individuals*, which has been edited for national use in this book. Dr. Taylor's inspiration and support throughout the development of the original guidelines were invaluable.

Dr. Taylor often commented that the guidelines developed in California reflected the ideas and work of pioneers in the education of visually impaired students in that state—Georgia Lee Abel, Florence Henderson, Berthold Lowenfeld, Dorothy Misbach, Pete Wurtzburger, and others. She would want these guidelines to be dedicated to them as well.

Contents

Foreword

Years ago, when people thought of blind children, they thought of residential schools and institutions. Today, nearly 90 percent of blind and visually impaired students are in their local schools along with their sighted peers. They are traveling independently and will be working in jobs that previously were unavailable to visually impaired persons. The education and preparation they receive have much to do with this kind of progress.

Program Planning and Evaluation for Blind and Visually Impaired Students: National Guidelines for Educational Excellence outlines what educational programs need to do to serve blind and visually impaired youngsters effectively.

It offers parents, teachers, administrators, and anyone involved in the education of these students information to help them make certain that the unique needs of these students are being met. We hope that the materials and resources presented here will contribute to the continued effectiveness of programs and services and the continued educational successes of blind and visually impaired young people.

William F. Gallagher
Executive Director
American Foundation for the Blind

Preface

In the early 1980s, the California legislature mandated the state's Department of Education to develop guidelines for programs serving deaf-blind, hearing impaired, severely orthopedically impaired, and visually impaired students. Jack Hazekamp, a consultant with the state's Special Education Division, was responsible for the development of the guidelines for services to visually impaired students, which were published as *Program Guidelines for Visually Impaired Individuals*. The talents and expertise of professionals and parents throughout the state were called upon in this effort, and the assistance of others from national blindness organizations was also requested. Kathleen Mary Huebner, then National Consultant in Education for the American Foundation for the Blind (AFB) was privileged to provide some input and was impressed by the scope of the guidelines, the thoroughness of the representation of the unique needs of blind and visually impaired students, and the clarity of presentation, all of which would ultimately lead to the guidelines' widespread use by special education personnel, regular education teachers, administrators, support personnel, and parents within California.

It is a formidable task to put into one document comprehensive guidelines for programs serving blind and visually impaired students, considering the multitude of elements involved in identification, assessment, program planning, implementation and evaluation, and appropriate and effective instruction on the elementary and secondary levels. Yet it was evident that the California effort met the challenge. Some states have developed guidelines, others are in the process of doing so, and still others have no such guidelines in written format to assist practicing administrators and teachers, new teachers to the state, and parents whose children are receiving educational services in a particular state.

AFB recognized the distinctive quality of the guidelines developed in California. Some of the characteristics, or particular strengths, of the guidelines that influenced AFB to adapt them for national use in the present volume were their readability and their appropriateness for teachers of visually impaired students, special education teachers, classroom teachers, special subject teachers, parents, support staff, rehabilitation counselors and teachers, transcribers, administrators, and anyone else involved in providing educational programs to blind and visually impaired students. California's guidelines were unique because they addressed study skills, affective education, descriptions of personnel that included roles and responsibilities, and a self-review guide that encourages readers to put the guidelines into action. But perhaps most important, the guidelines were child centered. It was obvious that blind and visually impaired students and their needs were kept in the forefront during the development of the guidelines, along with exemplary models of service delivery.

Based as it is on the guidelines developed in California, *Program Planning and Evaluation for Blind and Visually Impaired Students: National Guidelines for Educational Excellence* is the result of the work of all those initially involved in the development of the California guidelines. It is also the result of the additional direct efforts of Jack Hazekamp, Special Education Consultant, California State Department of Education and Dr. Kathleen Mary Huebner, Director of National Services in Education, Low Vision, and Orientation & Mobility for AFB, both of whom edited the original manuscript to broaden its application to national standards and reflect federal legislation and regulations; Natalie Hilzen, Managing Editor, AFB; and Mary Ellen Mulholland, Director of Publications and Information Services, AFB.

The role of the teacher of visually impaired students continues to be in transition. The job of this teacher is a demanding one, given the unique knowledge base and familiarity with a variety of service delivery systems that are needed and the heterogeneity of the students served. Teacher preparation programs grapple with decisions about which curriculum components to maintain and which ones to change to provide qualified teachers with the skills and confidence required to practice their profession and prepare students to take their rightful place in society. State certification requirements continue to need to be reviewed, modified, and standardized.

Although in recent years the federal government's education agency has supported a noncategorical approach to teacher training and certification, the program planning framework offered in this publication demonstrates the multiplicity of specialized skills that blind and visually impaired students need to learn and that are unique to them because of their sensory loss or limitation. It also demonstrates the multiplicity of specialized skills needed by teachers who work with these students. Parents, administrators, teachers, and rehabilitation personnel are encouraged to use this book to facilitate the planning and delivery of appropriate educational services and ensure optimal learning opportunities and experiences for blind and visually impaired students. The determination of factors such as type, frequency, and quantity of specialized services required by blind and visually impaired students should be based on thorough, timely assessments of students' needs, rather than on the availability of service delivery models. AFB believes that *Program Planning and Evaluation for Blind and Visually Impaired Students* will assist those who are involved in the education of blind and visually impaired students in their efforts to ensure an appropriate and effective education for all such students throughout the nation.

Susan Jay Spungin, Ed.D.
Associate Executive Director, Program Services
American Foundation for the Blind

Original Preface and Acknowledgments, *Program Guidelines for Visually Impaired Individuals*

A major responsibility of the Department of Education is to provide leadership and assistance to administrators, parents, and staff in their efforts to improve educational programs for the visually impaired at the local level. These guidelines have been developed by the Special Education Division of the Department to assist administrators, staff, and parents in improving the identification and assessment of the visually impaired and the planning and provision of instruction and services to these students.

Public education for visually impaired students in California has developed during more than 100 years, beginning with the establishment in 1860 of the California School for the Blind in San Francisco. The first public school program for visually impaired students was established in 1917; and the integration of students into regular school programs began in 1924, with the establishment of resource rooms for the visually impaired in elementary and secondary schools. Historically, California has been recognized as a leader in the education of visually impaired students through the innovative efforts of parents, staff, and administrators. We believe that this document will assist those who are continuing the efforts to meet federal and state legal requirements and to realize the dream of Helen Keller "that every blind child have an opportunity to receive a quality education."

Appreciation is extended for the contributions, advice, and assistance provided by the committee members who helped to prepare these guidelines and to the others who are identified in the acknowledgments. We are also grateful for the suggestions and reactions from those who reviewed early drafts and to Jack Hazekamp, Special Education Consultant, California State Department of Education, who coordinated the development of these guidelines.

Shirley Thornton
Deputy Superintendent
Specialized Programs

Patrick Campbell
Associate Superintendent and Director
Special Education Division

ACKNOWLEDGMENTS

These guidelines were developed with the assistance of an advisory committee representing a broad spectrum of individuals, organizations, and public and private agencies involved in the education of visually impaired students in California. This committee, listed below, provided an important link to the latest developments in this field and to the development of a document that is responsive to the needs of parents, teachers, and administrators.[1]

Linda Bourgaize, Director, San Benito/Santa Cruz Special Education Local Plan Area (SELPA)

Evelyn Carr, Consultant, Infant and Preschool Visually Impaired, California State Department of Education, Sacramento

Carol Chengary, Parent and President, California Association for Parents of the Visually Impaired, Northern California Chapter

Sandy Curry, Teacher and President, Northern California Chapter, Association for the Education of Visually Handicapped

Joy Efron, Coordinating Principal, Visually Handicapped Program, Los Angeles Unified School District

Jerry Fields, Program Director, Program I, Sonoma State Hospital

Robert Gordon, Optometrist specializing in low vision, Encino

Bruce Harrell, Chairperson, Joint Action Committee of Organizations of and Serving the Visually Handicapped

Lois Harrell, Home Counselor, Variety Club Blind Babies Foundation

Rona Harrell, Teacher representing the Southern California Chapter, Association for the Education of the Visually Handicapped

Philip Hatlen, Professor, Special Education Department, San Francisco State University

Mary Morrison, Director, Peninsula Center for the Blind, Palo Alto

Linda Roessing, Principal, California School for the Blind, Fremont

Ron Saviola, Doctoral Student, Physical Education/Visually Impaired, San Francisco State University

---

[1]The titles of the committee members were current as of 1984.

Jim Siegel, President, Southern California Chapter, California Association of Orientation and Mobility Specialists

Fred Sinclair, Director, Clearinghouse Depository for Handicapped Students, California State Department of Education, Sacramento

Judith Stotland, Parent and President, California Association for Parents of the Visually Impaired

Rose-Marie Swallow, Professor, Special Education Department, California State University, Los Angeles

Jeanne M. Vlachos, Superintendent, California School for the Blind, Fremont

The following served as consultants to the committee:

Gerald Breakstone, Ophthalmologist and Senior Medical Examiner, Los Angeles Unified School District

Eunice W. Cox, Consultant, Special Education Division, California State Department of Education, Sacramento

Carol Slavic, Member, Commission on Special Education; and Member, San Mateo County Board of Education

This document also reflects the valuable written comments and suggestions from the field and from meetings with parents, consumers, staff, and administrators representing the following agencies and organizations:

Butte County Special Education Local Plan Area (SELPA)

California School for the Blind, Fremont

Fresno Unified School District and county SELPAs

Los Angeles Unified School District and county SELPAs

Marin County SELPA

Monterey County SELPA

Organizations of parents of visually impaired children

Organizations of professionals serving the visually impaired

Organizations of the blind in California

Private agencies serving the visually impaired

San Benito/Santa Cruz SELPA

San Diego City Unified School District and county SELPAs

San Francisco Unified School District SELPA

Sonoma State Hospital

Special Education Administrators for County Offices

Special Education Local Plan Area Administrators

Yolo Country SELPA

Jack Hazekamp, Special Education Consultant, California State Department of Education, served as the chairperson of the advisory committee and coordinated and supervised the development of this document, with the valuable assistance of other departmental professional and administrative staff, particularly Allan Simmons, Administrator, Consultant Services South, Special Education Division, California State Department of Education. The clerical staff of the Special Education Division and the Word Processing Resources Center are also acknowledged for their efforts in the preparation of this publication.

A special appreciation is extended to Assemblywoman Gwen Moore, who sponsored the legislation requiring the development of guidelines for each low-incidence disability area.

Program Planning and Evaluation for Blind and Visually Impaired Students: National Guidelines for Educational Excellence

CHAPTER ONE

Purpose, scope, and use of the guidelines

Program Planning and Evaluation for Blind and Visually Impaired Students: National Guidelines for Educational Excellence was designed as a tool for those involved in planning and providing services to blind and visually impaired students. Parents or guardians, staff, and administrators were intended to be its primary audience. The standards and guidelines presented in this book represent research, legal requirements, and best practice in educational efforts, the intent being to improve the effectiveness of programs for blind and visually impaired students.

The national guidelines outlined here are based on *Program Guidelines for Visually Impaired Individuals,* which was published in 1986 by the California State Department of Education and revised in 1987. That publication was the result of a major effort that brought together parents, consumers, and leadership personnel from the field of education for visually impaired students to identify the components of educational services for youngsters with visual impairments. The product of this broad-based collaboration conducted in California has now been modified for national use.

The overriding rationale used in modifying the guidelines developed in California was to allow them to be used across the nation, regardless of geographic location. State-specific terminology and references have been replaced with those that have national recognition or represent policy of the American Foundation for the Blind (AFB). For example, references to the Special Education Local Plan Area (SELPA), the specific regional services delivery model used in California, were replaced with the more general term "regional special education agency," and the term "visually impaired," used in the original guidelines to refer to both functionally blind and low vision individuals, was often replaced in this publication by "blind and visually impaired" to acknowledge that all blind individuals are visually impaired but that all visually impaired persons are not blind. The first example demonstrates the effort to increase recognition and understanding by a national audience; the second reflects AFB policy. AFB editorial policy is also reflected in such changes as the use of certain acronyms, for example, the use of O&M for orientation and mobility.

Changes such as these appear throughout this book.

Various other editorial changes have been made. The "Self-Review Guide," formerly an appendix, has been given the status of a chapter in this publication because of its significance and its popularity among teachers, parents, and administrators. Other appendixes, such as those that identify resources, were altered to provide national information rather than information relating to an individual state. Appendixes that were specific to California have been replaced with those that address the same topics but present a national, rather than state, perspective. Several new appendixes and an annotated reading list have also been added.

PURPOSE OF THE GUIDELINES
The guidelines have been developed as a resource for parents, staff, and administrators in identifying and assessing the unique needs of visually impaired students and planning, providing, evaluating, and improving the quality and cost-effectiveness of programs serving these students. They are designed to
- Clarify the processes for the identification and assessment of needs and the planning and provision of instruction and services to meet the unique educational needs of visually impaired students
- Provide information that will assist parents, staff, and administrators in evaluating, improving, and maintaining effective programs
- Provide criteria for the self-review and monitoring of programs serving visually impaired students

The standards discussed in this publication were established in California to serve as a model framework of expectations for the provision of instruction and services for visually impaired students. Discussion includes the guidelines originally developed in California to assist local programs in meeting these standards.

It is recommended that individual states adapt the guidelines on the basis of their own legal requirements, funding models, and monitoring activities. State Departments of Education need to provide necessary technical assistance to parents, teachers, and administrators in implementing the guidelines.

ADAPTATION OF THE GUIDELINES

Although the guidelines originally formulated in California have been edited for use by other states and commonwealths, state and local education agencies may wish to adapt them further because of state-to-state variations in terminology, legal requirements, and monitor and review activities. In addition, individual states may wish to use a totally different format or to make major revisions in the material presented in this book. If this approach is used, it is recommended that a broad-based advisory committee be involved in the development of state-specific guidelines and that the guidelines of other states be studied.

It is further recommended that revisions, adaptations, or development of state-specific guidelines be coordinated by the state vision consultant, wherever possible. (See Appendix E for a discussion of the role of this consultant.) In states that do not have a vision consultant, the lead coordinator of efforts should be experienced in the education of blind and visually impaired students and skilled both in writing and in coordinating advisory groups. Technical assistance should be provided to parents, teachers, and administrators in implementing the state's guidelines, including workshops and in-service training on specific areas identified through a needs assessment. It is also recommended that the guidelines developed be incorporated into state monitor and review procedures for programs serving visually impaired students.

SCOPE OF THE GUIDELINES

The guidelines offered here focus on the unique educational needs of visually impaired students. All instruction and services provided to these students must be planned and coordinated to meet their needs. Close cooperation and coordination among all agencies, programs, and individuals assessing and providing instruction and services are the keys to meeting these needs successfully and to improving local programs.

The following areas of need are not included within the scope of this document unless they are affected by a student's visual impairment:

• Core curriculum, courses of study, proficiency standards, and standards of behavior and discipline. (It is expected that blind and visually impaired students should as much as possible have access to the core curriculum and meet the standards and expectations for all students.)

• Needs resulting from an additional disability or disabilities. (These needs are so varied and complex that they should be determined on an individual basis, using a multidisciplinary approach. See Appendix E for further discussion of services for students with multiple disabilities.)

• Other special needs, including those addressed by programs for bilingual, disadvantaged, migrant, and gifted and talented students. (These special needs are also complex, and they may or may not be affected by a student's visual impairment, depending on the individual student.) Persons needing more information about programs to meet other special needs may wish to contact their state Department of Education for technical assistance. (See Appendix C for addresses.)

USE OF THE GUIDELINES

This document was designed to be used in three major ways. First, the guidelines can help parents, staff members, and administrators improve their effectiveness in understanding and meeting the needs of visually impaired students. Recommended roles and responsibilities for parents, staff, and students appear in Chapter Four. Recommended roles and responsibilities for administrators are found in Chapter Five. These chapters include references to other sections in this publication that may be particularly helpful to these key individuals.

Second, the guidelines can serve as a tool for improving the effectiveness of programs in meeting the needs of visually impaired students and making maximum use of available resources. A discussion of program improvement is found in Chapter Five.

Third, the guidelines are a source of information and other resources to assist parents, staff members, and administrators in improving programs. The chapters in this book offer basic information and suggestions regarding the identification and assessment of educational needs and the provision of instruction and services to visually impaired students. The appendixes provide useful material on resources, funding, materials, and equipment; state Departments of Education; low vision assessment; and a range of other topics, including pertinent legal requirements.

ORGANIZATION OF THE GUIDELINES

Program Planning and Evaluation for Blind and Visually Impaired Students focuses on the unique educational needs of blind and visually impaired students and how programs can most effectively meet these needs. The organization of the book parallels the way in which programs should be organized around students' needs, and this is represented in Figure 1, which uses a series of concentric circles to show the relationships involved.

The unique educational needs of visually impaired students, the basis both of this book and of educational programs, are outlined in Chapter Two. This is represented by the center circle in Figure 1. The identification and assessment of these unique needs are the first

Figure 1. Organization of the guidelines

steps in developing educational programs; standards and guidelines for identification and assessment are presented in Chapter Three. These activities are represented as the first concentric circle in Figure 1. Students' assessed needs are in turn the basis for planning and providing instruction and services, as outlined in Chapter Four, which is represented by the second concentric circle in the figure. Organizing and supporting instruction and services based on assessed needs are necessary administrative components of programs, and guidelines for these activities are presented in Chapter Five, symbolized by the third concentric circle shown. Finally, program evaluation is essential in determining the effectiveness of educational efforts in all these areas; this important activity is the focus of Chapter Six and is represented by the outer circle in the figure.

STANDARDS FOR MEETING UNIQUE EDUCATIONAL NEEDS

The standards that appear in this book for meeting the unique educational needs of visually impaired students are based on research, legal requirements, and best practices. They are listed in the discussion that follows, and they are repeated in Chapters Three, Four, and Five, where they are accompanied by guidelines on ways to implement them. The standards are worded as statements of the characteristics that programs should have. Criteria for evaluating the effectiveness of programs in meeting each of these standards appear in Chapter Six, the "Self-Review Guide."

Standards in Chapter Three
- A program has procedures for locating and referring students with visual impairments who may require special education, including possible referrals from vision screening programs.
- The assessment of a student with a suspected visual impairment covers, where appropriate, the following areas related to the student's disability: vision/low vision, concept development and academic skills, communication skills, social/emotional skills, sensory/motor skills, orientation and mobility skills, daily living skills, and career and vocational skills.
- The assessment of visually impaired students is conducted by personnel who are knowledgeable about the disability.
- The assessment report identifies the student's unique educational needs related to the visual impairment, including needs for specialized equipment and materials.
- The persons assessing visually impaired students consider the variables that influence individual needs. These include, but are not limited to, variables related to congenital or adventitious visual impairments, the presence of multiple impairments, whether the child is an infant or of preschool age, whether the student is at the elementary or secondary level, the nature of the visual impairment, whether the student is functionally blind or has low vision, and whether the student has other special needs.

Standards in Chapter Four
- The assessed unique educational needs of visually impaired students form the foundation for developing the individualized education program (IEP) (mandated for each student by P.L. 94-142, the Education for All

Handicapped Children Act); for providing appropriate specialized instruction, services, materials, and equipment; and for developing curriculum in these areas: concept development and academic needs, communication instruction, social/emotional instruction, sensory/motor instruction, orientation and mobility instruction, instruction in daily living skills, and career and vocational instruction.

- The following key individuals who are involved in the identification and assessment of needs, the planning or provision of instruction and services, or consultation to visually impaired students understand the students' unique educational needs and possess the skills and abilities to carry out their roles and responsibilities in meeting these needs: teacher of visually impaired students, classroom teacher (regular, special class, or resource specialist); orientation and mobility specialist; parent, guardian, or conservator; visually impaired student; eye specialist; regular or adapted physical education specialist; occupational or physical therapist; school nurse; program specialist; specialist in career and vocational education; language, speech, and hearing specialist; counselor, psychologist, or social worker; transcriber; reader; aide; and ancillary staff in residential programs.
- Coordination exists among all the individuals involved in providing instruction and services to visually impaired students.

Standards in Chapter Five

- A program provides for the delivery of appropriate instruction and services through a full range of options established, as necessary, on a regional basis.
- Each visually impaired student is appropriately placed in the least restrictive environment on the basis of his or her educational needs.
- Class sizes and caseloads of staff allow for the provision of specialized instruction and services, based on the educational needs of visually impaired students.
- A program provides qualified staff who have the skills and abilities to conduct assessments and to deliver instruction and services that meet the educational needs of visually impaired students.
- Appropriate staff development and parental education are provided, based on a needs assessment that reflects the unique educational needs of visually impaired students.
- Facilities are designed or modified to enhance the provision of instruction and services to meet the unique educational needs of visually impaired students.

- Materials and equipment necessary to meet the unique educational needs of visually impaired students are provided, as indicated by the students' IEPs.
- Transportation for visually impaired students is suitable to the unique health and safety needs of these students.
- A program serving visually impaired students has an ongoing process to evaluate its effectiveness and improve the identification and assessment of needs and the planning and provision of instruction and services in meeting the unique educational needs of these students.

ADDITIONAL CONTENT

Chapter Six and Appendixes A through H provide additional information and sources of assistance for the reader. Chapter Six, the "Self-Review Guide," can assist parents, staff, and administrators in evaluating and improving the effectiveness of local programs in meeting the standards presented in earlier chapters. The "Self-Review Guide" can be used to

- Conduct an internal or external review of a program
- Identify areas and establish goals for program improvement
- Identify possible topics for local evaluation studies
- Identify needs for technical assistance.

Appendix A, "Resources for Technical Assistance," provides the names, addresses, and telephone numbers of organizations that can provide assistance and information nationwide. Appendix B, "Sources of Funding and Materials and Equipment," describes funding sources for low vision devices and funding for and sources of materials and specialized equipment for visually impaired students. Appendix C, "State Departments of Education," acts as a ready reference by listing the special education units or the state Departments of Education in every state and in the District of Columbia, Guam, Puerto Rico, and the Virgin Islands. Appendix D, "Assessing Vision/Low Vision," contains information about the range of visual impairments and the components of a functional vision assessment by a qualified eye specialist. This appendix also contains a variety of sample forms commonly used and encountered by parents and professionals.

The remainder of the appendixes provide supporting information from a variety of sources. Appendix E contains a sample of position papers developed and adopted by members of the Council for Exceptional Children, Division for the Visually Handicapped. These papers present explanations of the roles and responsibilities of teachers, state education consultants, instructional resource centers, and residential schools; the expanded role of the teacher of blind and visually impaired students who are multihandicapped; and parent-educator cooperative efforts. Appendix F contains an examination of ethical practices in providing services to blind and visually impaired infants and students. Appendix G deals with legal requirements and includes federal regulations from P.L. 94-142 and the California Education Code and California Code of Regulations. This appendix is meant to illustrate how one state responded to federal legislation and to assist residents of other states in comparing federal and state legislation and regulations. Appendix H provides an overview of P.L. 99-457, the amendments to P.L. 94-142 that deal with early childhood intervention. Each state has its own laws and regulations based on federal policy, and teachers, parents, and administrators are urged to obtain a copy of their own state's laws and regulations.

An annotated reading list and glossary are also provided for readers. The reading list describes a number of publications offering useful information for parents and professionals; the glossary contains definitions of terminology that appears in this book or that is used in educating visually impaired students.

CHAPTER TWO

Unique educational needs related to a visual impairment

The unique needs of blind and visually impaired students outlined here can be used as a general framework for assessing each student with a visual impairment and for planning and providing instruction and services to meet the assessed needs. These processes are described in Chapters Three and Four. In this chapter, students' unique educational needs are presented in relation to the following areas: concept development and academic skills, communication skills, social/emotional skills, sensory/motor skills, orientation and mobility (O&M) skills, daily living skills, and career and vocational skills. The information about educational needs offered in this chapter will provide valuable assistance for the team developing the individualized education program (IEP) and for those who implement the IEP.

CONCEPT DEVELOPMENT AND ACADEMIC NEEDS

A visual impairment will often impede a student's development of visual concepts and learning of academic subjects. Special concept development and academic skills, such as listening and study skills, will therefore often be needed.

Concept development and academic needs that should be addressed include:
- Developing a good sense of body image
- Understanding these concepts: laterality, time, position, direction, size, shape, association, discrimination, sequence, quantity, sensations, emotions, actions, colors (to the best of the individual's visual ability), matching, and classifying
- Developing listening skills appropriate to the level of the student's functioning, including the development of auditory reception, discrimination, memory, sequencing, closure, and association skills
- Developing auditory comprehension and analysis skills appropriate to the level of the student's functioning, such as the development of the ability to summarize; classify; compare; recognize cause and effect; predict outcomes; visualize; understand character; understand setting; recognize climax, foreshadowing, and purpose; and distinguish fact from opinion

- Becoming familiar with the format of, and knowing how to use, reference materials in the student's primary reading medium
- Being able to interpret accurately maps, charts, graphs, models, and tables
- Developing writing and recording skills for note taking during lessons
- Developing skills for note taking from material originally intended for print, for example, from recorded material or material read aloud
- Developing the ability to organize notes and other study materials
- Developing the ability to organize one's time
- Developing the ability to select and use a reader
- Being able to acquire material in the appropriate reading media, such as braille or large type.

COMMUNICATION NEEDS

A student with a visual impairment will usually require alternative modes for instruction in reading and writing. He or she will need special skills in using alternative strategies and specialized equipment and materials to communicate effectively.

Communication needs that should be addressed include:
- Being skilled in reading, using appropriate modes (for example, braille or print and recorded form) for such purposes as gaining academic information and pursuing personal, career, and recreational interests
- Developing skill in writing for personal, academic, and career needs, using appropriate modes (braille, print, typewriting, recording, and/or handwriting) for such purposes as note taking, recording phone numbers and addresses, taking messages, and recording travel directions and personal notes
- Being proficient in typing
- Being able to write one's own signature legibly
- Being able to operate basic communication equipment, such as radios, talking book machines, reel-to-reel tape recorders, cassette recorders, and phonographs
- Being cognizant of and able to use appropriate special devices for reading and writing, such as slates and styli, braillers, prescribed optical devices, closed-

circuit television systems, talking computers, reading machines, and other electronic equipment
- Being cognizant of and able to use appropriate special devices for mathematics and science, for example, the abacus, talking calculators, paperless braillers, specialized measuring equipment, and talking computers.

SOCIAL/EMOTIONAL NEEDS

A visual impairment often affects a student's self-concept, observation of behavior in social situations, involvement in recreational activities, and sexuality. Blind and visually impaired students will, therefore, have special needs for socialization, affective education, recreation, and sex education. They will also need to learn to deal with the psychological implications of their visual impairments.

Socialization

Socialization needs that should be addressed include:
- Understanding and displaying acceptable social behavior appropriate to a variety of group situations
- Being able to discriminate between behaviors not socially acceptable in public but acceptable in private
- Understanding and exhibiting appropriate assertiveness in a variety of situations
- Being aware of and using appropriate techniques in verbal communication, such as the use of voice volume and intonation
- Being aware of and using appropriate techniques in nonverbal communication, such as the use of gestures, eye contact, and facial expressions
- Being aware of and being able to control body posture, movement, and physical mannerisms in an appropriate, coordinated manner
- Being aware of and using proper manners in eating and in social situations
- Being able to make introductions properly and demonstrate appropriate conversational skills
- Being prepared to contribute constructively to group activities and social situations
- Being aware of appropriate social distances in which to communicate with others
- Being aware of dress codes for specific groups and occasions and dressing appropriately for one's age and situation.

Affective education

Affective education needs that should be addressed include:

- Recognizing that each person is unique and different from every other person
- Understanding that visually impaired persons have all the same emotions as everyone else
- Being able to identify one's feelings
- Being able to express one's feelings to others directly and in a socially acceptable manner
- Having feelings of self-worth and well-being
- Recognizing one's own strengths and weaknesses in a realistic manner
- Acknowledging both positive and negative feelings in oneself and in others and understanding that both types of feelings are legitimate
- Being able to identify and appropriately express one's likes and dislikes
- Being able to understand and recognize teasing and sarcasm and developing appropriate ways of handling them
- Being aware of alternative ways to respond to the feelings and behavior of others
- Feeling that one is a valuable, contributing member of society
- Being able to identify and understand a wide range of feelings in oneself and in others, including happiness, guilt, frustration, boredom, confusion, anger, embarrassment, and pride
- Being aware that the way a person feels about himself or herself is reflected in the way he or she treats others
- Being aware that each person must establish his or her own set of values and live by them
- Being aware of the concept of peer pressure and determining the appropriateness of conforming to such pressure
- Being able to identify and share feelings about one's visual impairment in relation to being accepted by peers
- Understanding the ways in which people can become victimized by allowing others to make choices for them
- Understanding the long-range results of too much dependence on others
- Being able to feel comfortable asking for or refusing help when it is appropriate
- Understanding the difference between allowing others to help when it is not needed and deciding to ask for help when it is needed
- Being aware of the connection between being in control of one's life and taking responsibility for what happens to oneself in life.

Recreation

Recreation needs that should be addressed include:

- Being familiar with a variety of social and recreational activities
- Being able to participate in a variety of recreational activities with a group and on an individual basis
- Realizing that many options are involved in deciding how to spend one's leisure time
- Learning to play indoor and outdoor games appropriately, for example, ball, cards, and roller skating
- Developing hobbies of individual interest, such as arts, crafts, or music
- Being competent in several different recreational activities
- Learning about popular spectator activities in order to enjoy attending them and being able to discuss them appropriately
- Being aware of opportunities for participation in recreational activities in the neighborhood and the community in addition to those designed specifically for visually impaired people, such as neighborhood parks and centers, scouting, school and social clubs, and the Young Men's (or Women's) Christian (or Hebrew) Association
- Being aware of current recreational trends and being able to participate when appropriate, such as in current dance steps or currently popular games.

Sex education
Sex education needs that should be addressed include:
- Being able to identify with one's own gender
- Recognizing that each human being is a sexual entity and has certain characteristics associated with gender
- Identifying sexual roles in our society
- Understanding what constitutes a family and the various roles of family members
- Being aware of the stages of the life cycle
- Having knowledge of the reproductive process in a variety of living things
- Being aware of the factors that influence the growth of one's body
- Being aware of the biological and emotional changes that occur in human males and females during puberty
- Understanding that differences occur in the rate of maturity of individuals' bodies
- Being knowledgeable about appropriate grooming and personal hygiene techniques
- Being able verbally and tactilely, with the use of models, to identify the body parts and organs of the reproductive systems of human males and females, using correct terminology

- Being able to use correct terminology to explain how sexual intercourse and human fertilization occur
- Being aware of the changes in the human body during pregnancy and the developmental process of the growth of the fetus
- Being aware of the birth process and possible complications in the process
- Being knowledgeable about the factors that should be considered during pregnancy to increase the chances of delivering a healthy baby
- Being knowledgeable, through contacts with real infants and children, about appropriate child care procedures and adaptations that may be necessary for a visually impaired parent
- Being knowledgeable about available options in family planning
- Being aware of the common types of venereal diseases, their symptoms and consequences, and preventive measures and treatments
- Being aware of appropriate dating and social mores to be used with the opposite sex, such as flirting or asking someone for a date or to dance
- Being aware of the various types of interpersonal relationships one can have with members of the opposite sex
- Being aware of verbal and nonverbal communications that relay sexual messages to others, for example, the use of body language
- Being knowledgeable about strategies for the prevention of sexual and physical abuse, including inappropriate touching and verbal advances, and rape
- Understanding that there are individuals with different types of sexual preferences
- Being knowledgeable about the genetic factors related to some visual impairments that one might consider before having children, and being aware of genetic counseling
- Being aware of the responsibilities associated with premarital sexual relations, marriage, and parenthood
- Being able to express and discuss concerns related to one's visual impairment and relations with the opposite sex, such as feelings about dependency, not being able to drive, financial concerns, and genetic factors.

Psychological implications
How well a student understands and accepts his or her visual impairment can be determined by addressing the needs in this area, including:
- Being able to recognize that one has a visual impairment

- Being knowledgeable about one's own eye condition
- Being able to explain one's eye condition to others
- Understanding how vision works
- Understanding and accepting any physical limitations caused by one's visual impairment
- Understanding how low vision devices can help improve visual abilities and accepting the use of appropriate low vision devices
- Accepting the use of alternative techniques and apparatuses for obtaining sensory information where appropriate, for example, the use of braille, tapes, and the long cane
- Being knowledgeable about the elements of personal eye care, including medications, hygiene, regular eye exams, and low vision assessments
- Having realistic knowledge of current research and treatment as they relate to one's visual impairment.

SENSORY/MOTOR NEEDS

A visual impairment may affect a student's gross and fine motor skills, alternative sensory discrimination and sensory integration skills, and abilities to develop appropriate posture, balance, strength, and movement. Blind and visually impaired students may need to develop special skills in these areas.

Sensory/motor needs that should be addressed include:

- Learning to control the head, limbs, and body for purposeful exploration and movement
- Learning to sit, crawl, stand, and walk independently
- Learning to control the head and body while sitting, crawling, standing, and walking, exhibiting appropriate gait, stride, and mannerisms
- Developing the ability to balance while standing still and while in motion
- Using gross motor skills, such as those used in crawling, walking, exploring objects, negotiating stairs, negotiating depth changes, opening and closing doors, and pushing and pulling objects
- Developing fine motor skills, such as those used in grasping and releasing objects, turning door handles, grasping a cane, and dialing a phone
- Developing sufficient muscle relaxation and flexibility to perform basic daily living and mobility skills safely, efficiently, and gracefully
- Developing sufficient strength, stamina, and endurance to complete tasks involved in routine mobility, physical education, and daily living skills
- Learning to identify, discriminate, and use various tex-

tures and objects tactilely, with the feet and other appropriate parts of the body
- Learning to identify, select, discriminate, track, and use continuous and intermittent auditory sources of information indoors and outdoors, including direct, indirect, and reflected sound sources
- Learning to identify, discriminate, and use various kinesthetic and proprioceptive sources of information indoors and outdoors, such as changes in temperature, movement of air currents, or height of slopes and depth changes
- Learning to identify, discriminate, and use various olfactory sources of information indoors and outdoors.

ORIENTATION AND MOBILITY NEEDS

A visual impairment usually affects how a student learns about and functions within various environments. Visually impaired students, therefore, will need special skills to understand and become oriented to environments and to move, travel, and play independently and safely within them. O&M needs that should be addressed include:

- Developing a conceptual understanding of body image as well as comprehension of concrete environmental concepts, spatial concepts, compass directions, and concepts relating to traffic and traffic control. *Body image* involves such concepts as planes, parts, laterality, and directionality in relation to objects and environmental features. *Concrete environmental concepts* relate to such items as grass, lawn, cement, wood, carpet, tile, tree, bush, street, curb, and intersection. Examples of *spatial concepts* include far, near, close, high, low, above, below, facing, in front of, behind, beside, away from, next to, forward, backward, sideways, and 90, 180, and 360 degree turns. *Compass directions* relate to such concepts as relationships involving north, south, east, and west; sides of streets; names of corners; and relationships among changes in direction. *Traffic and traffic control concepts* include fast, slow, parallel, perpendicular, same direction, opposite direction, near side, far side, stop signs, walk signs, and light-controlled intersections.
- Learning to crawl, stand, and walk independently
- Learning to identify, discriminate, and track increasingly complex auditory, tactile, kinesthetic, or olfactory cues
- Learning to travel independently at home
- Learning to control the head and body to exhibit comfortable and appropriate gaits and strides
- Learning to control the head and body to exhibit

appropriate physical mannerisms while standing still, moving, and sitting

- Learning appropriate trailing and protective techniques and techniques for locating objects to facilitate independent O&M at home and school
- Learning to use appropriate sighted guide skills in all travel situations when needed, such as traveling in normal situations; going through narrow passages; being on ascending and descending stairways, on escalators, on elevators, and outdoors; switching sides; seating oneself in chairs, on sofas, and at tables; and establishing and maintaining control of the sighted guide situation with familiar and unfamiliar guides
- Learning to use vision as well as distance low vision devices, as appropriate, to the maximum extent possible for independent, safe O&M
- Learning to travel independently at various school settings throughout one's school career
- Learning to use the long cane appropriately to supplement or replace visual travel skills (skills to be acquired are basic grasp and hand and arm position; touch technique; use of the cane at closed doorways, with stairs, in congested areas, and in social situations; trailing techniques; and modified touch technique for snow travel and location of drop-offs like curbs or down staircases)
- Developing a level of maturity sufficient for understanding the importance, dangers, responsibilities, and appropriate behavior of independent travel in increasingly sophisticated settings
- Learning to become oriented and to travel independently in urban, suburban, and rural areas (examples of skills in this area are traveling along a residential sidewalk); traveling past driveways and walkways; locating curbs and wheelchair ramps; recovering from veering; crossing residential streets; recognizing and recovering from a change in direction in street crossings; using tactile, auditory, kinesthetic, or olfactory environmental cues, compass directions, maps, and spatial relationships for orientation and safe mobility in familiar urban, suburban, and rural areas; and becoming oriented independently to an unfamiliar area)
- Developing an understanding of the services various business establishments provide, for example, grocery stores, department stores, post offices, shopping malls, and banks
- If nonverbal, developing a feasible communication system for acquiring information and communicating needs

- Learning to use adaptive mobility aids, if necessary, such as wheelchairs, walkers, braces, and orthopedic canes, to provide for the maximum amount of independent mobility possible
- Being able to develop and travel alternate routes and, if necessary, specific routes in limited areas to care for basic needs as independently as possible
- Learning the skills necessary to become oriented and to travel independently in small and major metropolitan business areas:
  —Using traffic sounds to establish, maintain, or regain orientation and line of travel
  —Traveling safely and appropriately on busy sidewalks in business areas
  —Crossing independently intersections of four lanes or more controlled by traffic lights
  —Exhibiting appropriate verbal and physical public behaviors
  —Developing the ability to seek out and interact appropriately with the public to obtain assistance in orientation or mobility as needed
  —Learning to use community address systems as an aid to orientation
  —Carrying identification and emergency funds when traveling
  —Knowing whom to contact in case of emergency or disorientation
  —Knowing how to locate and use a pay telephone (dial or push-button)
  —Learning to locate independently various destinations in business areas
  —Learning to travel safely in various retail and service establishments, including independent travel on escalators and elevators
  —Learning to carry out increasingly complex personal business transactions independently
  —Understanding and being able to use public transit systems
  —Learning to acquire information regarding products, services, and location of various stores and businesses by using the telephone, including recording this information for later referral
  —Being able to recognize and safely travel past areas of road construction
  —Being able to negotiate railroad track crossings independently
  —Being able to travel independently within business areas at a level sufficient to carry out tasks necessary for basic survival.

DAILY LIVING SKILLS NEEDS

A visual impairment affects a student's ability to live independently, and visually impaired students will often need to learn special techniques to function as independently as possible. Assessment and instruction regarding daily living skills should include the following areas:

Personal hygiene skills
- Performing basic personal hygiene tasks, such as tending to toileting, care of teeth and hair, and bathing needs
- Using personal service businesses to care for one's own needs and making necessary appointments, such as with a barber or beauty shop (these activities are for students who are beyond the basic skill level).

Dressing skills
- Dressing and undressing, including tying shoes and fastening buttons and zippers
- Selecting appropriate clothing and planning purchases of clothing.

Clothing care skills
- Using techniques for storing clothing and identifying colors and patterns and for sorting laundry and using a washer and dryer
- Using services such as shoe repair, performing minor repairs on clothing, and hemming and ironing clothing.

Housekeeping skills
- Locating and using housekeeping areas in the home, such as the kitchen, dining area, and bedroom, and assisting in basic upkeep by doing such tasks as putting out trash and setting the table
- Performing many basic housekeeping tasks, such as vacuuming and scheduling regular maintenance
- Being able to make basic home repairs.

Food preparation skills
- Identifying kitchen appliances and performing basic techniques of pouring, stirring, measuring, and spreading
- Using kitchen equipment, such as a stove, preparing menus, following recipes, and preparing meals.

Eating skills
- Locating food on the plate
- Using utensils properly; being familiar with passing food to others or conveying it to oneself, serving oneself at buffets, and using cafeterias; ordering food from restaurant menus; and understanding tipping.

Money management skills
- Identifying and knowing coin equivalents
- Handling money in public, planning a budget, using checking and savings accounts, and having one's own system for money management.

Social communication skills
- Conducting basic social interactions, including communicating one's needs
- Conversing appropriately with familiar persons and strangers.

Skills in telephone usage
- Identifying one's own telephone number and placing an emergency call
- Using directory assistance and various types of telephones for personal and business calls, arranging for one's own telephone service, and displaying good telephone etiquette.

Written communication skills
- Understanding that written communication is used to convey information and ideas
- Writing a signature and personal and business letters, using a system for recording information, and ordering basic office supplies correctly.

Time monitoring skills
- Responding to and being able to follow a daily schedule and knowing events that occur during the daytime versus the evening
- Knowing how to tell time and use clocks and watches, understanding the passage of time and such concepts as weeks and months, scheduling one's own time, and keeping appointments.

Organization skills
- Organizing time and activities systematically
- Arranging and organizing personal belongings.

CAREER AND VOCATIONAL NEEDS

Visually impaired students will often need guidance in selecting an appropriate career. Assessment and instruction in career awareness and special vocational education skills, including adaptive skills, will often be required by an individual for success in a chosen career.

Career and vocational needs that should be addressed include:
- Understanding oneself in terms of the characteristics

and attributes that contribute to one's individuality and recognizing one's uniqueness as a person with a visual impairment

- Understanding that a variety of lifestyles is acceptable
- Knowing the difference between work and play and when each is appropriate
- Relating present experiences to future jobs
- Being familiar with jobs held by one's family members and the jobs available in the school and community, including jobs held by visually impaired persons
- Being able to fill out a job application or give the necessary information to another person
- Being familiar with the development and use of a résumé
- Knowing basic skills and factors relating to employability, including getting to work on time
- Knowing that money is a medium of exchange and related to work and developing concepts of financial management
- Developing competencies in decision making
- Knowing and using personal information skills, including how to write a legal signature

- Understanding the importance of doing a job to the best of one's ability, of becoming employed to increase one's self-esteem, and of interacting appropriately with supervisors
- Maximizing one's capabilities in manual skills, including the use of basic tools, with the goal of using the hands to explore and control the environment
- Participating in hands-on work experiences through chores, through paid jobs on or off campus or after school (particularly in the private sector), or in simulated work environments
- Participating in skills training at an entry-level job in a variety of experiences to help determine realistic occupational choices
- Being able to serve as one's own advocate in obtaining necessary services, adaptations, and equipment needed for success on a job, during job training, or in college.

(For additional information on the areas discussed in this chapter, see the "Selected Reading List.")

CHAPTER THREE

Identifying and assessing unique educational needs

To be eligible for special education and related services in a particular state, a student must meet the state's specific requirements. These requirements can be obtained from the local education agency or special education division of the state's Department of Education. In P.L. 94–142 regulations, the federal government defines a visual impairment as one that "even with correction, adversely affects a child's educational performance." Many states use a modification of the federal definition, which is applied in a variety of ways. In California, for example, students who have visual impairments and who, after a comprehensive assessment, are found to have educational needs that cannot be met without special education and related services are to be provided with instruction and specialized services, materials, and equipment in accordance with an individualized education program (IEP). (See Appendix G.)

In general, for educational purposes, the term "visually impaired" includes the following:

- Functionally blind students (who rely basically on senses other than vision as their major channels for learning)
- Low vision students (who use vision as a major channel for learning).

A visual impairment does not include visual perceptual or visual motor dysfunction resulting solely from a learning disability.

The standards that appear in this chapter relate to the identification of visually impaired students and the assessment of their unique educational needs. The standards are worded as statements of the characteristics that programs should have and are designated in italics throughout.

IDENTIFICATION OF VISUALLY IMPAIRED STUDENTS

STANDARD: A program has procedures for locating and referring students with visual impairments who may require special education, including possible referrals from vision screening programs.

Identifying a student's visual problems at an early age is critical. Local procedures to find these students should include search activities, such as the following, to locate and refer individuals suspected of having a visual impairment:

- Coordination with local vision screening programs
- Organization of activities to make staff members and parents aware of signs that may indicate a student has a visual impairment
- Coordination with eye specialists and other possible referral sources. (See Appendix A for sources of referral information and Appendix D for assessment information.)

ASSESSMENT OF VISUALLY IMPAIRED STUDENTS

STANDARD: The assessment of a student with a suspected visual impairment involves, where appropriate, the areas related to the student's disability. (These areas are specified below.)

To identify all the unique educational needs of a student resulting from his or her visual impairment, those assessing the student must be sure that the initial comprehensive and ongoing assessments address, where appropriate, the areas that are outlined in Chapter Two. (See Appendix G for legal requirements and Appendix D for information that will be helpful in assessing a student's vision/low vision.) Various aspects of the assessment of visually impaired students are described in the discussion that follows.

Reports on vision

Assessment of a student should begin with the report of an examination by an ophthalmologist or optometrist. It is important that as much information as possible be acquired from the eye specialist and that parents and/or the teacher of visually impaired students who may accompany the child during the eye specialist's examination communicate effectively with the specialist. The specialist's findings may be reported in the "Eye Report for Children with Visual Problems" form produced by the National Society to Prevent Blindness or in other educationally oriented vision reports. Sample copies can be found in Appendix D.

The eye report should indicate the following:

- Near and distant acuity, with and without best possible correction

- Field of vision, including peripheral field
- The etiology and prognosis of the visual impairment
- The eye specialist's recommendations for school personnel and parents, including an indication of when the student should be reexamined.

Cooperation among parents, teachers, and eye specialist is critical during eye examinations of severely multiply impaired students, whose vision may be difficult for an eye specialist to assess because of problems in obtaining accurate communication between the child and the specialist. Further information for assessment can be obtained from the student's pediatrician or from other attending medical staff. Information can also be obtained through electrodiagnostic testing (for example, visually evoked response testing) and functional vision assessments.

A state-accepted eye report is also used as the basis for registering visually impaired students annually with the state. This registration provides for the use of materials, devices, and equipment produced by the American Printing House for the Blind. (See Appendix B.)

Low vision
For a visually impaired student with low vision, it is strongly recommended that a low vision assessment be provided in accordance with the guidelines that follow. In the first step, a functional vision assessment is conducted by a teacher of visually impaired students in coordination with the orientation and mobility (O&M) specialist and the student's parents, to determine the student's functional vision. (Appendix D contains more detailed information and a sample report form.) Parents can provide valuable information on how the student uses his or her vision.

The purposes of the functional vision assessment are to accomplish these ends:
- Determine what the visually impaired student sees functionally in a variety of settings and situations
- Indicate modifications required for visual efficiency, such as task modifications, including time requirements; specialized instructional materials and equipment; and desired seating, lighting, and physical arrangements
- Facilitate further assessment by an eye specialist, when necessary
- Complement the needed interdisciplinary exchange of information between educators and eye specialists.

In the second step, recommendations from the functional vision assessment report are made to the assessment team or IEP team regarding the possible need for further assessment by a licensed optometrist or ophthalmologist who has training and expertise in low vision, has appropriate low vision devices and assessment equipment available, and provides follow-through. Referral to a low vision clinic and resulting findings and recommendations may be useful.

When the assessment of a student with low vision is to be discussed, the assessment team or IEP team, or both, should include the individuals who conducted the functional vision assessment. When a recommendation is made for further low vision assessment, the assessment team or IEP team, or both, should include an individual knowledgeable about prescriptive low vision devices and additional low vision assessment. The information from the low vision assessment will be extremely useful in determining the needs of the student in other areas related to the visual impairment.

Concept development and academic skills
Although assessment and instruction in academic subjects are the major responsibilities of the classroom teacher, visually impaired students should be thoroughly assessed by a teacher of visually impaired children (vision teacher), in coordination with the classroom teacher, in academic areas such as mathematics, reading, and language arts (particularly spelling). Such assessments will not only provide valuable information about the level on which a student is performing academically but will also provide the teacher of visually impaired students with an opportunity to observe how the student functions visually or tactilely in regard to academic tasks. When an assessment indicates that a student's errors are the result of unique educational needs related to his or her visual impairment, intervention by the teacher is necessary.

Vision is the major channel through which sighted students perceive their environment and the relationship of themselves and objects within it. Functionally blind and low vision students, therefore, often require appropriate instruction in concept development to progress from understanding concrete and functional levels of information to comprehending abstract levels of instruction. Assessment should, therefore, include the student's understanding of these basic concepts:
- Spatial concepts
- Temporal concepts
- Quantitative concepts
- Positional concepts
- Directional concepts
- Sequential concepts.

Because visually impaired students must rely on their auditory sense for learning to a greater degree than their sighted peers do, an assessment of the student's listening skills should also be conducted, including the student's auditory perception, comprehension, and skills of analysis. Study skills should also be assessed, such as the following:

- Using reference books and materials
- Interpreting maps, charts, graphs, and models
- Taking notes from both written materials and oral presentations
- Keeping one's place
- Tracking
- Comprehending the "whole," based on observations of the "parts."

Communication skills

Good communication skills are essential for a student's successful integration into the school and later into society. The assessment of a visually impaired student's communication skills should begin with an evaluation of the reading (braille, large print, print, or aural) and writing (braille, print, cursive, or aural) modes being used by the student. The teacher of visually impaired children, with suggestions from the student when possible, should determine whether these modes are the most appropriate for the student at that particular time or whether other (or additional) ones should be introduced.

Once the student's reading and writing modes have been determined, the efficiency and accuracy with which the student performs in them should be assessed to determine whether further instruction is necessary to improve his or her technique, speed, or accuracy. In addition, skills in the following areas should be assessed where appropriate:

- Typing
- Signature and cursive writing
- Familiarity with basic communication equipment, such as Talking Book machines, tape recorders, reading machines, and radios
- Computers and computer adaptations
- Optical aids
- Closed-circuit television systems
- Braille/slate and stylus and brailler
- Abacus
- Talking calculator
- Other equipment specially designed or modified for visually impaired students.

Social/emotional skills

The assessment of the social and emotional skills of a visually impaired student encompasses the areas of socialization skills, affective education, recreation, human sexuality, and the psychological implications of the student's visual impairment. Various formal and informal methods of assessment exist with which the teacher of visually impaired students is familiar, and these are used to assess skill levels in each of these areas. The development of positive social and emotional skills is essential for the student's ability to function independently at home, at school, and as an adult and to be effective in employment and interpersonal relationships.

Sensory/motor skills

The development of sensory/motor skills is essential if the student is to benefit from instruction in O&M, daily living skills, prevocational and vocational skills, and physical education. Various formal and informal assessment methods exist with which the teacher of visually impaired students and the O&M specialist are familiar.

Orientation and mobility skills

The development of O&M skills is essential if the visually impaired student is to travel independently in various community settings. The needs of visually impaired students in this area are unique because vision loss requires them to learn and travel about their environment in a way different from that of sighted students. Assessments should address how the visual impairment affects the student in regard to the following areas of functioning:

- Understanding of the physical environment and space
- Orientation to different school and community environments
- Ability to travel in school and around the community
- Ease of finding opportunities for unrestricted, independent movement and play.

Daily living skills

If a visually impaired student is to function independently at home and at school and as an adult, development of daily living skills is essential. An individual's ability to become independent will vary. The needs of each student must be assessed and instruction provided so that he or she has the opportunity to learn as many independent living skills as possible.

The assessment of daily living skills often requires a careful task analysis of the skill being evaluated because prerequisite learning may not have occurred. In addition, a student's level of ability in the assessed skill should be precisely specified in terms of the level of assistance the student needs to complete the skill.

Career and vocational skills

Employment should be viewed as an important goal for each visually impaired student. The development of concepts in this area begins in early childhood, and assessment and training must begin early and progress through four sequential stages: awareness, exploration, preparation, and participation.

Assessing and addressing a student's needs in all of the other areas related to his or her disability are important, because these needs relate directly to the student's ability to make a successful transition from school to the world of work. Assessments of the student's needs for career and vocational education programs should include consideration of his or her prevocational skills (including work habits, attitudes, and motivation), vocational interests, and vocational skills. Assessment of needs and the training required to meet these needs will be aimed at developing the skills necessary for a range of employment possibilities.

ASSESSMENT PERSONNEL

STANDARD: The assessment of visually impaired students is conducted by personnel who are knowledgeable about the disability.

To be knowledgeable about the disability of visual impairment, the persons conducting the assessment of visually impaired students must have the following:

- The necessary training and materials to assess the cognitive, affective, social, and motor abilities of visually impaired students
- A familiarity with tests designed and those adapted for visually impaired individuals
- An awareness of the availability of large-print and braille assessment materials.

Communication among persons who will assess the visually impaired student, including comments from the teacher of visually impaired students and recommendations from the parent and student, should precede the assessment so that the most effective method of nondiscriminatory testing can be established. Throughout the assessment, the teacher should be involved in identifying areas that should be addressed. These include but are not limited to the following factors:

- Use of nondiscriminatory assessment instruments, as required by state and federal law
- Need for additional testing time by the student
- Visual performance of the student
- Low vision devices, if needed

- Previous assessments
- Lighting requirements
- Print and picture size appropriate for the student
- Best positioning of materials
- Other assessment strategies
- Motivation of the student
- Other special needs, for example, those of bilingual students.

Assessments must be administered by qualified individuals so that the desired data and educationally relevant information are obtained. Assessment instruments that require specific technical skills for their administration, such as intelligence (IQ) tests, should be undertaken by qualified psychologists. Teachers can use many formal and informal assessment tools and administer, score, and interpret these instruments. The teacher of visually impaired students should be a valuable resource person. When formal assessment tools are administered, it is important that the manual of directions be understood and carefully followed. It is often helpful to other professionals, such as school psychologists and physical or speech therapists, if the teacher is available or works cooperatively in the preparation of the visually impaired student for testing, in the actual administration of the assessment, and in the interpretation of assessment results.

ASSESSMENT REPORT

STANDARD: The assessment report identifies the student's unique educational needs related to the visual impairment, including needs for specialized equipment and materials.

The unique educational needs of each visually impaired student that have been identified in the assessment, including needs for materials and equipment, should be included in an assessment report. Assessment reports can be helpful in the coordination of all the assessments conducted by the multidisciplinary team. The unique educational needs, as well as the strengths identified in the reports, will provide valuable information, which should be used to develop or review a student's IEP.

VARIABLES AFFECTING EDUCATIONAL NEEDS

STANDARD: The persons assessing visually impaired students consider the variables that influence individual needs. (A listing of these variables follows.)

When assessing the unique educational needs of each student and providing instruction and services, staff must consider the variables that influence individual needs. These include but are not limited to variables related to visually impaired students who fall into these categories:

- Have a congenital or adventitious visual impairment
- Have multiple impairments
- Are infants or preschool children
- Are at the elementary or secondary level
- Have varying degrees of visual impairment
- Are functionally blind or have low vision
- Have other special needs.

Congenital or adventitious visual impairment

The terms *congenital* and *adventitious* refer to the time of onset of a visual impairment. A congenitally visually impaired student has had a visual impairment since birth or early infancy and generally has difficulty with concepts and skills that are visual in nature. An adventitiously visually impaired student has a visual impairment that was acquired after visual memory was established and has some visual concepts and skills. This student may need to integrate visual concepts and concepts learned through other sensory input and may have needs relating to his or her adjustment to the visual impairment.

Students with multiple impairments

The unique educational needs of visually impaired students with one or more additional impairments are diverse and complex. Personnel who work with students with complex needs resulting from multiple impairments should:

- Use a multidisciplinary team approach in assessing and providing instruction and services to meet students' needs
- Coordinate assessment, as well as instruction and services, through ongoing communication among all other personnel serving the students, to ensure that all needs are met.

In using the team approach to assessment and instruction, it is important to include specialists with expertise in all the student's disabilities. (See Appendix E and Appendix F.)

Infants and preschool children

Visually impaired infants and preschool children have distinctive educational needs. Until these individuals have developed complex mental processing abilities, a difficult task without vision, they are surrounded by sounds, smells, and sensory perceptions that have little or no meaning to them.

Opportunities for learning, such as opportunities to make associations among sounds, shapes, and objects and their purposes, a process that often occurs incidentally with sighted children, must be directly provided. Because research shows that the first five years of a child's life are the most important for developing a foundation for learning, special emphasis must be given to the infant and preschool child whose opportunities to learn through visual observation are limited or nonexistent.

Assessment should include but not be limited to these areas:

- Potential for delays in development and learning because of limited experiential opportunities in specific areas. These include sensory/motor development, communication skills development, cognitive development, daily living skills development, and social/emotional development, including the development of self-concept and self-esteem.
- Acceptance of the family as the primary provider of experiential and learning activities
- Opportunities for family members to learn from qualified personnel the way in which they can assist the child's learning
- Provision for the integration of concepts and the ability to generalize
- Provision, through early and appropriate introduction to educational processes, for a smooth transition from preschool services to elementary school services.

In general, the guidelines described for school-age children also apply to infants and preschool children. (See Appendix G and Appendix H for legal requirements in this area.)

Elementary and secondary school students

Elementary and secondary school students who are visually impaired require a special curriculum to address their unique educational needs (identified in Chapter Two) so that they may have equal access to the district (or local education agency), or core, curriculum. These students' needs can be met in specific ways to accomplish this goal.

Elementary school students. Students in an elementary school program may have needs in areas described in the previous section, "Infants and Preschool Children," particularly if they have developmental delays or have not received needed instruction and services as infants or at the preschool level. Elementary school students should be provided intensive instruction in the basic skills that they need to function independently in the regular classroom. Often, these students should be placed in a resource room for visually impaired students, especially in the primary grades, to receive such instruction. (See Chapter Five for a discussion of placement in the least restrictive environment.)

Elementary school students should receive instruction and services that will prepare them for secondary school. Developing career education and prevocational skills, addressing prescribed courses of study, and meeting state and local standards should be areas of concern. These students also need instruction in accepting responsibility for their educational needs.

Secondary school students. Students in a secondary school program should be encouraged to become increasingly responsible for their educational needs, including obtaining necessary adapted classroom materials and equipment and selecting and using readers. These students should receive instruction and services that focus on skills enabling them to function independently as adults, particularly career-related and vocational education skills.

Secondary school students should, to the extent possible, meet the requirements of the prescribed course of study and state and local standards for graduation. When appropriate, as determined by the IEP team, these students should use alternative means (such as more time) or modes (such as large type or braille) to meet standards.

The nature of the visual impairment
A student's unique educational needs will be influenced by the cause or type of vision loss as well as by the student's age at the onset of the visual impairment. The following two points should be noted about visual impairments in general:

- Students' visual impairments range from mild, moderate, or severe impairment to functional blindness. (See Appendix D for a discussion of visual impairments.)
- The visual status of an individual student may be stable, fluctuating, slowly or rapidly deteriorating, or subject to improvement.

Functionally blind and low vision students
Functionally blind students will have needs related to the use of their other senses as primary channels for learning. Braille reading and writing are particularly important. Students should not rely solely on their minimal vision when it is not efficient or effective for reading or writing.

Low vision students will have needs related to the use of their vision as a primary channel for learning. Information derived from a low vision assessment will be particularly useful in identifying and meeting these needs. (See Appendix D for information on low vision assessments.)

Students with other special needs
Some students will have other special needs that should be considered during assessment. Examples of students with other special needs are those who are bilingual or limited in their English proficiency, gifted, educationally disadvantaged, or at risk because of specialized health care needs; living in threatened home environments; or members of migrant families. Those conducting assessments of students with other special needs must work closely with staff from programs and agencies providing services to meet these needs. For example, when a visually impaired student whose primary language is not English is being assessed, materials in the appropriate language and medium should be obtained and prepared, and a translator should be provided when the teacher or the O&M specialist does not speak the child's primary language.

CHAPTER FOUR

Planning and providing instruction and services

P lanning and coordination are crucial factors in the provision of instruction and services. The standards that appear in this chapter relate to assessment of unique needs as the foundation for educational activities, the roles and responsibilities of key individuals in meeting these needs, and the coordination of instruction and services to meet these needs. The standards are designated in italics throughout.

UNIQUE EDUCATIONAL NEEDS
STANDARD: The assessed unique educational needs of visually impaired students form the foundation for these important activities:
- Developing the individualized education program (IEP), which includes, when appropriate, specialized services and materials and equipment (See Appendix G for legal requirements.)
- Providing appropriate instruction, services, materials, and equipment
- Developing curriculum and implementation strategies to meet these needs.

Concept development and academic needs
For most visually impaired students, it is expected that information in core curriculum areas will be obtained as a part of instruction in the classroom. The classroom teacher, the visually impaired student, and the teacher of visually impaired students should all work closely together to ensure that concepts that may be unfamiliar (for example, contractions of words in reading braille, mathematics, and columns) or visual demonstrations (for example, science experiments and examples on the chalkboard) do not slow the integrated student's progress and ability to keep up with the rest of the class. If the visually impaired student also has a learning handicap, the resources of a specialist in that area should be used so that the student may perform to the maximum level of his or her ability. Three areas in which visually impaired students may require specialized instruction are concept development, listening skills, and study skills.

Concept development. The development of concepts in sighted children is based almost entirely on their visual observations of the world. This process involves the identification of objects, the relationship of children to objects in their environment, and their conceptualization of the relationships among objects. Unless these relationships are specifically taught, they cannot be totally understood by students whose visual perceptions are distorted. A comprehensive, sequential program of concept development is necessary for most visually impaired children before they can be expected to develop abstract thinking skills.

Listening skills. Individuals who are functionally blind or have low vision do not automatically develop better listening skills; these must be systematically taught and practiced. The development of good listening skills does not stop with work in auditory perception but extends to auditory comprehension, analysis, and memory skills. In particular, good listening skills will be needed by the student to interpret the environment when the student works in the regular classroom, when books and other materials are read to the student (by a reader or on tape), or when the older student tries to retain the maximum amount of information from lectures.

Study skills. The study techniques used by visually impaired students are so different from those used by sighted students that study skills should be taught by a specialized teacher of visually impaired children. The various formats used in reference works, such as dictionaries, encyclopedias, and atlases, coupled with the complexity of tracking and keeping one's place in these books, demand that special attention be given to the development of specific skills.

Reading and interpreting maps, charts, and graphs also require special techniques, whether the material is in braille or large print or is being read using an optical device. Also, visually impaired students need to develop methods of taking notes while listening or reading and to organize notes and other materials in media that they can use. In addition, they should develop the skills needed to acquire and use a reader.

Communication instruction
Without communication skills, individuals cannot be fully independent and must therefore rely on others to assist them at home, at school, at work, and in society. For the

visually impaired individual, dealing with information in a written form is particularly difficult. Unique problems arise both in the reception of printed material (reading) and in the written transmission of one's thoughts and opinions (writing). Many visually impaired students will need special instruction in one or both of these areas to develop proficiency in communication.

Reading techniques are not acquired for sighted and visually impaired individuals in the same manner. Depending on the visual functioning of the student, special instruction in reading techniques for braille, large print, or regular print may be necessary. For written communication, depending on the student's visual functioning, use of a braillewriter, slate and stylus, pen and pencil, typewriter, and/or electronic equipment should be taught.

Social/emotional instruction

The social and emotional needs of visually impaired students are unique because of the effects that a lack or loss of vision may have on the formation of one's self-concept, opportunities for appropriate modeling in social situations, involvement in recreational activities, development of concepts about human sexuality, and understanding and awareness of one's visual impairment. Needed skills and understanding in these areas should be addressed to help visually impaired students develop the appropriate social and emotional skills necessary to function independently at home and in school as adults in vocational, interpersonal, and family relationships.

Socialization. Visually impaired students often have needs in regard to the development of appropriate social skills. The majority of a sighted person's social skills are learned from visual modeling. That is, an appropriate behavior or mannerism is observed and then is copied in a similar situation. Many acceptable social behaviors go unnoticed by visually impaired students unless they are taught these behaviors with an appropriate demonstration of the behavior and an explanation of when and why one would behave in this way.

Visually impaired students have other needs regarding socialization because the area of nonverbal communication is often inaccessible to them. Nonverbal ways of communicating are frequently critical avenues of social interaction for sighted people and must be directly addressed if visually impaired students are to incorporate them into their repertoire of social skills.

Affective education. The emotional needs of visually impaired students must be addressed through affective education so that these needs do not interfere with students' academic, social, and career or vocational growth. A crucial emotional developmental task for visually impaired students is the formation of a self-concept. Research has shown that visually impaired children and adolescents do not have as accurate a self-concept as their sighted peers.

Visually impaired infants and young children often have difficulties in recognizing themselves as individuals apart from other individuals and objects in the environment, because vision plays such a crucial role in this differentiation process. The lack of feedback from a mirror, which assists sighted students in learning how they appear to others, further hinders the development of a healthy self-concept in visually impaired students.

As visually impaired students become older, they may perceive themselves as devalued or incapable persons because of their inability to perform many of the common tasks required in school or on the playground. Another common occurrence is the visually impaired student's overemphasis of certain strengths, which may result in an unrealistic self-concept that can later be deflated in adolescence or adulthood. Visually impaired students also often encounter teasing by peers and must learn to handle such situations constructively while maintaining a good self-concept. In addition, many emotional issues arise when the visually impaired student reaches adolescence. Among these issues are dealing with learned helplessness, dependency, overprotective families, and sexuality.

Recreation. Students with visual impairments are often limited in the range of recreational and leisure-time activities, including extracurricular activities, that are available to them. These students should be exposed to a variety of available options, which they may not be aware of or about which they may not feel competent.

The sighted person becomes aware of many recreational activities through visual sources not available to the person with a visual impairment. Many specific leisure skills are learned from visual modeling, which visually impaired students may not be able to do. In addition, visually impaired students may be limited because of a lack of mobility skills, and they cannot always independently explore neighborhood options. For these reasons, both individual and group recreational activities must be included in efforts to help students develop recreational skills, including skills in art and music.

Human sexuality. Visually impaired students need a much more intensive and conceptually oriented sex education program than their sighted peers do. Often, they lack conceptual understanding and accurate information because they cannot gain them through the visual media available to sighted students. Many times visually impaired students can verbalize sexual concepts and information accurately, but further inquiry reveals that they have many misconceptions.

The use of anatomically correct tactile models is an important part of the sex education programs for visually impaired students because visual media are not useful to them in the learning process. Dealing with the attitudes and emotions surrounding these students' sexuality at various stages of growth is important. The confusion that often exists regarding the stigmas attached to the disability and sexuality of visually impaired individuals can seriously affect the self-concepts of students.

Existing local sex education programs should be adapted for visually impaired students so that gender identity, reproduction processes, sexual and social issues, and health and safety precautions are dealt with—all in relation to each student's visual impairment and moral code. Before sex education is provided, both the IEP and local policies and procedures should be followed.

Psychological implications of the visual impairment. Many of the psychological problems faced by visually impaired students stem from a lack of understanding and acceptance of their eye condition. Many students cannot discuss their eye problem when others inquire about it. Visually impaired students are often uncomfortable discussing their vision problems, since such a discussion forces them to acknowledge that they do, in fact, have a visual impairment. These students need to understand and embrace fully their visual impairment as part of their identity so that a healthy adjustment results and they are able to deal with the stereotypes and prejudice often encountered in our society. If students are knowledgeable and comfortable about and accepting of their visual impairment, their chances of creating a similar comfortable and accepting attitude in others will increase.

Sensory/motor instruction

From an early age, sighted children are able to use vision, imitation, and opportunities for unrestricted exploration, movement, and play to develop necessary fundamental skills in the following areas: gross and fine motor coordination, relaxation of muscles, strength, endurance, flexibility, and balance. Sighted children also are better able to develop their tactile, auditory, proprioceptive, and kinesthetic sense discrimination and integration. The lack of visual, imitative, and normal play opportunities

may hinder the ability of visually impaired students to develop these fundamental skills through the natural process of development and maturation or as a result of regular physical education activities.

Instruction in development or remediation of identified needs in the area of sensory/motor skills should be provided, as needed, by a team of instructional personnel that may include the classroom teacher, special class teacher, teacher of visually impaired children, physical education teacher, adapted physical education specialist, orientation and mobility (O&M) specialist, occupational therapist, and physical therapist. Sensory/motor development needs overlap with several other areas of need. In some cases, certain skills and abilities are prerequisite to the development of more sophisticated skills in other areas, particularly O&M, daily living skills, and career and vocational education.

Orientation and mobility instruction

The ability to understand, interact with, and move within one's physical and spatial environment is a fundamental developmental skill. This ability is one of the milestones indicative of maturation for sighted students and should be so viewed for visually impaired students as well.

A visual impairment may affect an individual's opportunities for unrestricted, independent exploration, movement, and play; understanding of the physical environment and space; ability to become oriented to and to travel in various community environments; and ability to acquire basic daily living and social skills necessary for interaction with sighted individuals and for travel within the school and the community. A visual impairment may also result in voluntary or imposed restrictions on a person's activity that are imposed simply because of the presence of a visual impairment and associated misconceptions about the ability of students to develop independent movement capabilities.

Specific instruction and services will be necessary to meet students' assessed needs in the following areas:
- Environmental and spatial concept development, body image, control, and purposeful movement
- Orientation techniques
- Adaptive visual or nonvisual mobility techniques
- Use of residual vision for travel or orientation
- Daily living skills related to community travel and independence.

For reasons of safety and liability, persons providing O&M instruction must be qualified. For example, instruction in the use of the long cane and off-campus instruction should be provided only by a qualified O&M specialist.

Instruction in daily living skills

Specific instruction in daily living skills will often be necessary if visually impaired students are to function independently at home, at school, and later as adults. Sighted children learn these daily living skills from their parents beginning at a very early age. Parents of visually impaired students are often unaware of the students' ability to acquire these skills or are reluctant to teach them because they usually have not had any training in the use of adaptive techniques.

For sighted children, the acquisition of daily living skills, for example, eating and dressing independently or doing household chores, is seen as a developmental milestone. Often, visually impaired students are not expected to be independent in this area, which results in their performing daily living skills at a level far below the level of skills expected from sighted students. Working closely with parents and other caretakers as early as possible is important so that they can assist in teaching these skills and following through at home. One of the most effective ways of teaching daily living skills is through involvement of the parents by providing instruction, as appropriate, in the student's home.

For sighted children, many skills of daily living are learned incidentally or reinforced through visual modeling. Depending on the level of visual functioning of a visually impaired student, he or she should be taught these skills through the use of specialized or adapted skills and equipment.

Teaching students to make simple adaptations so that they will be able to function independently in a variety of settings and situations is important. Planning, instruction, and curriculum should focus on self-help needs of increasing complexity within each of these areas of daily living skills: personal hygiene, dressing, clothing care, housekeeping, food preparation, eating, money management, social communication, telephone use, written communication, time, and organization.

Career and vocational instruction

Career and vocational education is an essential component in programs for visually impaired students. Even though new technology and legislation that prohibits discrimination have provided more opportunities for employment, visually impaired individuals will continue to encounter many barriers in realizing their employment potential. Career and vocational education should therefore begin early and continue through four phases: awareness, exploration, preparation, and participation.

Awareness. Awareness begins during early childhood and includes the development of a person's self-esteem and self-concept and the beginning of an understanding of how people live, work, and play. Activities at this level should begin to assist students to develop a realistic self-appraisal of their skills, abilities, attitudes, and strengths, as well as their limiting factors. Instruction should also help students gain the skills, abilities, and attitudes they need to become successfully employed. Awareness also includes an introduction to the world of work and occupations, in which those positions that are held, or could be held, by visually impaired individuals are emphasized.

Exploration. Exploration should begin when students have developed a realistic awareness of their abilities and limitations as well as their interests. The consideration of employment that might appear to require vision should not automatically be eliminated. Instead, students should be encouraged to explore ways, including the use of technology, in which the occupational tasks involved could be adapted for a visually impaired person. Rehabilitation counselors from state and private rehabilitation agencies and other individuals knowledgeable about employment opportunities and adaptations for visually impaired people need to be involved.

Preparation. Preparation should include vocational training in the specific skills, abilities, and attitudes necessary for the individual's success in his or her field of interest or choice. A student should become a client of the state rehabilitation agency no later than the tenth or eleventh grade or after reaching a comparable chronological age.

Participation. Participation can include on-the-job training for a specific career or work experiences that will provide opportunities for students to develop the skills, abilities, and attitudes that will be valuable in any career choice. Cooperation with local vocational education programs is essential, including sheltered workshops, supported work programs, regional occupational programs and centers, and local businesses. Knowledge of individual rights and affirmative action policies, current law, and the skills of self-advocacy should also be included in a career and vocational education program.

Career-related areas of learning and achievement are lifelong activities for everyone. Because visually impaired students are unable to learn about them through visual observation, as sighted students do, the training of students with visual impairments to meet their career and vocational needs should receive special emphasis.

Materials and equipment

To provide instruction and services to meet the assessed needs already described, a program must supply, as indicated by students' IEPs, materials and equipment, ranging from braille and large type to recordings, tactile diagrams, and electronic devices. If a student's IEP so indicates, certain materials and equipment must be provided.

Those responsible for providing materials and equipment for students should follow these guidelines:

- Functionally blind students will need tactile or auditory adaptations, or both, in the form of braille, recorded materials, and technological devices in order to function optimally within a classroom.
- Low vision students will often be able to use regular or large type as their primary reading medium, even though the use of adaptations such as low vision devices (for example, magnifiers or closed-circuit television) may be necessary. Recorded materials, technological devices, and braille may also be needed.
- Multiply impaired students with visual impairments will need to use a wide variety of materials and equipment, depending on the combination and severity of their impairments. For multiply impaired students who need a specialized curriculum, the standard adaptations (braille, typewriter, large type, and so forth) may be used as modes for learning. Students may need additional time to master the operation of equipment and the use of materials.
- Nonacademic students, infants, and preschool children will need to use concrete objects, picture representations, auditory and tactile materials, and so forth to enhance sensory stimulation, concept development, and readiness skills. (See Appendix B for information on sources of funding and materials and equipment.)

ROLES AND RESPONSIBILITIES OF KEY INDIVIDUALS

STANDARD: The key individuals who are involved in the identification and assessment of needs, the planning or provision of instruction and services, or consultation to visually impaired students understand the students' unique educational needs and possess the skills and abilities to carry out their roles and responsibilities in meeting these needs.

The skills, abilities, and knowledge of the individuals involved in the assessment or provision of instruction, services, or consultation to visually impaired students should be examined. Each IEP specifies the special education instruction and services, including specialized services, materials, and equipment, needed by a visually impaired student. (See Appendix G for legal requirements.) The degree of coordination that can be achieved among all the individuals involved in implementing the IEP, and the knowledge and skills of these individuals, will play a vital role in the success of the total program in meeting all the needs of the student. Therefore, each person who provides instruction and services to visually impaired students must understand his or her roles and responsibilities, including ethical responsibilities. (See Appendix F.) The remainder of this chapter lists these individuals and outlines the functions they perform.

Teacher of visually impaired students

The teacher of visually impaired students has the following roles and responsibilities:

- Has primary responsibility for specialized instruction and services required to meet the unique educational needs of the visually impaired student
- Possesses the skills and abilities necessary to provide and coordinate this specialized instruction
- Assists the student, parents, special and regular education personnel, and the student's sighted peers in (1) understanding the unique educational needs and learning characteristics of visually impaired students, (2) becoming aware of services and support available from local programs for visually impaired students, (3) acquiring information regarding local, state, and national resources for the education of visually impaired students, and (4) interpreting the visually impaired student's specific eye condition, the educational implications of the visual impairment, and the results of functional vision assessments
- Confers regularly with the classroom teacher, other regular and special education personnel, parents, and others to coordinate programs and services for the visually impaired student
- Assists the site administrator and teachers in making environmental adjustments for the student in the school and in the improvement of practices and procedures
- Shares responsibility with classroom teachers in the identification of instructional areas in which the student requires assistance
- Has responsibility for selecting and obtaining large-type or braille textbooks, supplementary materials, educational aids, and equipment needed by the visu-

ally impaired student and the classroom teacher to ensure the student's maximum participation in all classroom activities (appropriate educational materials may be prepared or adapted by the teacher of visually impaired students, or they may be obtained from educational, clerical, or transcriber services)

- Provides specialized instruction to the visually impaired student, school personnel, and parents in the use of necessary educational aids and equipment
- Provides instruction to the visually impaired student in the development and maintenance of skills designed to meet the student's unique educational needs in these areas, as indicated in the IEP: (1) low vision and visual efficiency skills in coordination with the eye specialist, (2) concept development and academic skills in coordination with the classroom teacher and other staff, (3) communication skills in coordination with the regular teacher and the language, speech, and hearing specialist (these skills include braille reading and writing as appropriate), (4) social/emotional skills and abilities in coordination with counselors, psychologists, and classroom teachers, (5) sensory/motor skills in coordination with the physical education instructor, occupational and physical therapist, and O&M specialist, (6) daily living skills in coordination with the O&M specialist, classroom teacher, and parent, and (7) career and vocational education skills in coordination with career and vocational education staff and rehabilitation counselors
- Provides assistance to the classroom teacher in academic subjects and activities of the classroom that, as a direct result of the student's visual impairment, require adaptation or reinforcement for the student
- Provides assistance in any assessment
- Conducts the functional low vision assessment in coordination with the O&M specialist
- Attends IEP meetings for students with visual impairments
- Shares responsibility for initial and ongoing assessments, program planning, and scheduling with parents, the student when appropriate, the classroom teacher, principal, counselor, and other school personnel
- Schedules adequate time for assessment, instruction, planning, preparation of materials, travel, and conferences with relevant school and other key individuals (scheduling should be flexible to meet the varying needs of each student)
- Maintains ongoing contact with parents to assist them in the development of a realistic understanding of their child's abilities, progress, and future goals

- Provides in-service training programs for all school personnel and students and education for parents regarding the needs of visually impaired students and adaptations, programs, and services for these students
- Is aware of pamphlets, films, and other public information materials that may be useful in developing realistic and unprejudiced attitudes toward visually impaired students
- Assists in the coordination of other personnel, such as transcribers, readers, counselors, O&M specialists, career/vocational education staff, and rehabilitation counselors
- Maintains a reference library of current professional materials
- Acquires information about current research, development, and technology.

In a self-contained classroom or school for visually impaired children, the teacher of visually impaired students may be responsible for instruction in all subjects in addition to undertaking most of the previously listed responsibilities. (See Appendix E for further discussion of the role of this teacher.)

Classroom teacher

The classroom teacher (regular, special class, or resource specialist) has the following roles and responsibilities:

- Provides instruction to the visually impaired student in the classroom
- Works cooperatively with the teacher of visually impaired students to (1) identify the visually impaired student's areas of educational need, including unique educational needs, (2) coordinate instruction and services to meet these needs, (3) provide, in a timely manner, the teacher of visually impaired students with classroom materials that need to be reproduced in another medium, (4) determine mutually convenient times during the school day for scheduling the teacher of visually impaired students to work with the student, (5) modify classroom procedures and environment to meet the specific needs of the visually impaired student for participation in classroom activities, and (6) exchange information concerning the visually impaired student with parents and other individuals on a regular basis.

Orientation and mobility specialist

The O&M specialist has the following roles and responsibilities:

- Instructs the visually impaired student in the development of skills and knowledge that enables him or her to travel independently to the highest degree possible, based on assessed needs and the student's IEP

- Teaches the visually impaired student to travel with proficiency, safety, and confidence in familiar and unfamiliar environments
- Provides consultation and support services to parents, regular and special education teachers, other school personnel, and sighted peers
- Confers regularly with parents, classroom teachers, physical education teachers, and/or other special education personnel to assist in home and classroom environmental modifications, adaptations, and considerations and to ensure reinforcement of appropriate O&M skills that will encourage the visually impaired student to travel independently in these settings
- Works with the teacher of visually impaired students to conduct the functional vision assessment as it relates to independent travel
- Conducts assessments that focus on both long-term and short-term needs of the student
- Includes in the assessment report the needs and strengths of the student and an estimate of the length and frequency of service necessary to meet identified needs
- Prepares sequential and meaningful instruction geared to the student's assessed needs, IEP goals and objectives, functioning level, and motivational level
- Prepares and uses equipment and materials, for example, tactile maps, models, distance low vision devices, and long canes, for the development of O&M skills
- Transports the student to various community locations, as necessary, to provide meaningful instruction in realistic learning environments
- Is responsible for the student's safety at all times and in all teaching enivronments while fostering maximum independence
- Evaluates the student's progress on an ongoing basis
- Keeps progress notes on each student
- Participates in necessary parents' conferences and meetings
- Provides in-service training to regular and special education personnel, sighted peers, and parents concerning the O&M needs of the visually impaired student and appropriate methods and procedures for interacting with the visually impaired person that will foster maximum independence and safety

- Provides O&M instruction, where appropriate, in a number of specific areas. These are
  — Body imagery
  — Laterality
  — Environmental concepts
  — Gross and fine motor skills related to independent travel
  — Sensory awareness, stimulation, and training
  — Spatial concepts
  — Compass direction concepts
  — Sighted guide procedures
  — Basic protective and information-gathering techniques
  — Orientation skills
  — Map skills
  — Cane skills
  — Use of residual vision
  — Low vision devices related to travel skills
  — Urban, suburban, and rural travel
  — Travel in business districts
  — Procedures for crossing streets, including how to deal with traffic control signals
  — Use of public transportation systems
  — Procedures for use of the telephone for information gathering and for emergencies
  — Procedures for interacting with the public
  — Knowledge and application of community address systems
  — Procedures for travel and independent functioning in places of public accommodation
  — Skills of daily living
  — Sensory/motor skills in coordination with the physical or occupational therapist and teacher of visually impaired students.

Parent, guardian, or conservator

The parent, guardian, or conservator has the following roles and responsibilities:

- Is fully informed as to why an assessment is being conducted and how it is to be conducted
- Provides information relating to the assessment, including medical information
- Gives informed written consent before an individual assessment is conducted and receives a copy of the assessment report when he or she requests it
- Is knowledgeable about the assessment results prior to the IEP meeting in order to participate more effectively in the meeting
- Participates as a member of the IEP team by stating observations about the needs and interests of and

expectations and goals for the child, cooperating with school and other personnel to determine IEP goals and objectives for the child, and accepting responsibility for assisting in the implementation of IEP goals and objectives

- Participates in ensuring that an appropriate educational program is planned and implemented to meet the individual needs of the child and maintains communication with school personnel to accomplish this goal, including providing feedback and suggestions about the instruction and services being provided
- Provides, in cooperation with school personnel, an appropriate educational program in the home to improve the student's daily living skills, career and vocational skills, O&M skills, and other developmental skills as a supplement to special instruction and services to meet the child's unique educational needs
- Provides ideas for and participates in formal and informal parental education programs designed to assist parents in understanding and meeting the needs of visually impaired children
- Has information and assistance from school personnel and other sources to acquire the knowledge and skills necessary to participate in meeting the unique educational needs of the child. (See Appendix A for various sources of information and Appendix E for discussion of parent/educator efforts.)

Visually impaired student

The visually impaired student has the following roles and responsibilities:

- Is involved, unless it is clearly not appropriate, in all decisions about his or her education
- Is encouraged to provide information about his or her unique educational needs, strengths, and expectations as part of assessment
- Participates, when appropriate, in the development of the IEP
- Gives feedback and suggestions about the instruction and services being provided
- Has high expectations and works toward achieving them to become as independent as possible.

Eye specialist

The eye specialist, a licensed ophthalmologist or optometrist, makes vision-related recommendations to the classroom teacher, teacher of visually impaired students, O&M specialist, and other professional staff. Some ophthalmologists and optometrists specialize in low vision impairments and have the necessary equipment and expertise to assess low vision and prescribe low vision devices. (See Appendix D for more detailed information.)

Regular or adapted physical education specialist

The regular or adapted physical education specialist has the following roles and responsibilities:

- Is knowledgeable about unique educational needs in the area of sensory/motor skills
- Works closely with the teacher of visually impaired students, the O&M specialist, and the occupational or physical therapist to share needed information and coordinate services that may be provided by these individuals
- Is familiar with specialized or adapted equipment for visually impaired children in the area of physical education
- Involves students in appropriate physical education activities that can be applied in daily life.

Occupational or physical therapist

The occupational or physical therapist has the following roles and responsibilities:

- Is aware of unique educational needs of visually impaired individuals, particularly in the area of sensory/motor skills
- Works closely with the teacher of visually impaired students, the O&M specialist, and physical education staff to coordinate services.

School nurse

The school nurse has the following roles and responsibilities:

- Acts as a liaison with health professionals, educators of visually impaired children, other school personnel, and parents
- Coordinates screening of vision and hearing, including making referrals and screening the hearing of visually impaired students
- Provides assistance in determining the need for additional health assessments, for example, physical examinations or referrals to other agencies
- Cooperates with the teacher of visually impaired children in teaching visually impaired students about specialized health care needs, such as how to insert eyedrops and how to care for, insert, and remove prosthetic eyes.

Program specialist

The program specialist has the following roles and responsibilities:

- Has in-depth knowledge of visually impaired students'

unique educational needs and experience in providing education for these students

- Provides technical assistance and in-service training to all personnel working with visually impaired students and their parents
- Is knowledgeable about local, state, and national resources for visually impaired persons
- Is especially knowledgeable about program options and services available locally or regionally.

Specialist in career and vocational education

The specialist in career and vocational education has the following roles and responsibilities:

- Is aware of unique educational needs in career and vocational education and other related areas and appropriate career and vocational assessment tools
- Consults and works cooperatively with the teacher of visually impaired students, the O&M specialist, and parents in determining realistic goals and instruction in these and related areas
- Is knowledgeable about the expanding career and vocational education opportunities currently available to visually impaired individuals, including the use of technological devices
- Coordinates efforts with the rehabilitation counselor or counselor/teacher in the local office of the state rehabilitation agency.

Language, speech, and hearing specialist

The language, speech, and hearing specialist has the following roles and responsibilities:

- Is aware of the visually impaired student's functional vision and unique educational needs in the areas of communication (particularly language development), concept development and academic skills, and sensory/motor skills
- Works closely with the teacher of visually impaired students to coordinate instruction and services.

Counselor, psychologist, or social worker

The counselor, psychologist, or social worker has the following roles and responsibilities:

- Is aware of the unique educational needs of the visually impaired student or the student's family
- Works closely with the teacher of visually impaired students to coordinate services
- Is knowledgeable about special considerations for visually impaired students when conducting assessments. (See Appendix G for legal requirements.)

Transcriber (certified braille specialist/recorder)

The transcriber (certified braille specialist/recorder) has the following roles and responsibilities:

- Holds Library of Congress certification for preparing materials in braille
- Adheres to standards of the Braille Authority of North America when preparing braille materials in literary braille, mathematics, music, foreign languages, or computer notation
- Is knowledgeable about embossing tools, techniques, and media and understands the concepts to be presented when preparing tactile materials
- Adheres to the transcribing standards and procedures for large type of the National Braille Association and qualifies as a typist according to the standards of the local educational agency when preparing materials in large type
- Has the necessary competencies to prepare aural media, including knowledge of recording equipment, the ability to comprehend and present materials at an appropriate pace, and a well-modulated voice.

Reader

The reader has the following roles and responsibilities:

- Possesses the skills necessary to read print materials to visually impaired students, including knowledge in the use of recording equipment; good articulation and pronunciation and a pleasant voice; ability to follow the directions of the teacher and student; and ability to meet deadlines
- When the reader is a student or volunteer, works under the supervision of the teacher of visually impaired students.

Aide

The aide has the following roles and responsibilities:

- As directed by the teacher of visually impaired students or other credentialed staff, assists in (1) facilitating the organization of the classroom and other environments, (2) reinforcing the individualized instruction provided by the teacher to achieve IEP goals and objectives, and (3) planning and preparation of materials
- Is familiar with the unique needs of students in the class.

Ancillary staff in residential programs

The roles and responsibilities of staff members will vary, depending on the agency in which they work:

- Dormitory and other residential care personnel, including staff in state hospitals/intermediate care facilities, are responsible for the health, safety, and well-being of students when they are not in school. Since these staff members engage in activities with students similar to those normally provided by parents, these personnel should be aware of the unique needs of students and coordinate their efforts with those of instructional staff, particularly in the area of daily living skills, so that consistency in expected behavior occurs.

- Food service staff members are responsible for planning, preparing, and serving meals to students. Diets should be monitored so that they meet the special needs of students. Food service staff should coordinate their activities with those of instructional staff, when appropriate, in reinforcing students' eating skills.
- Health services staff members are responsible for the health and medical needs of students and should communicate with appropriate personnel regarding the changing health and medical needs of students, particularly concerning medications and special health care needs.

COORDINATION OF INSTRUCTION AND SERVICES

STANDARD: Coordination exists among all the individuals involved in providing instruction and services to visually impaired students.

To be effective, all instruction and services should be coordinated to focus on the visually impaired student. Meetings concerning the IEP and the educational program itself should form the foundation for the coordination of instruction and services.

It is important, however, that all key individuals who are involved develop formal and informal ways of communicating with one another on an ongoing basis to ensure that the IEP is implemented in a coordinated manner. Since many key individuals are often involved in the education of visually impaired students, one staff member should be assigned to facilitate this coordination among all parties, including the parent. In most cases, the teacher of visually impaired students will have this responsibility when the visual impairment is the student's primary disability. (See also Appendix E for discussion of the role of the state education consultant.)

CHAPTER FIVE

Organizing and supporting instruction and services

Organizing and supporting teaching efforts and other related services involve attention to a large variety of elements. The standards that appear in this chapter relate to such important factors as regionalization, least restrictive environment, class sizes and caseloads, and staff development and parent education. The standards are designated in italics throughout.

REGIONALIZATION
STANDARD: A program provides for the delivery of appropriate instruction and services through a full range of options established, as necessary, on a regional basis.

The concept of regionalization is particularly important for programs serving visually impaired students because these students constitute a low-incidence or low-prevalence group that is small in size and spans a wide range of ages. New programs for visually impaired students should be planned and existing programs modified so that instruction and services necessary to meet these students' varied and unique educational needs, including the provision of essential materials and equipment, can be delivered through coordinated administrative services on a regional basis.

To provide needed instruction and services in an efficient and cost-effective manner, staff members from the special education arm of the local education agency (LEA) may find it necessary to cooperate with adjacent local education agencies and states, particularly in rural areas. Collaborative efforts could include districts, counties, intermediate units, and other regional special education agencies as defined by the state's annual program plan, which is submitted to the federal government as required by P.L. 94-142. Local or regional plans are also required by some states. (A state's Department of Education can be contacted for information on the given model used in the state; see Appendix C for addresses.) Other options include contracting with private agencies for services, teleconferencing, and using staff members who are dually certified teachers.

Because of the importance of coordination in these efforts, it is essential that roles and responsibilities be examined for staff of regional special education agencies and for key administrative personnel as well. Each state's

annual program plan outlines the roles and responsibilities for the specific regional special education model used within the state as well as local education agencies. Regardless of the model used, responsibility for provision of and consultation to special education programs and support services for visually impaired students must be clearly defined, including, when necessary, provisions for coordinating efforts with other agencies and states. The roles and responsibilities of the supervisor of personnel serving visually impaired students and the site administrator or designee, two key persons, are outlined in the sections that follow.

Supervisor of personnel serving visually impaired students
The supervisor of personnel serving visually impaired students has the following roles and responsibilties:

- Is knowledgeable about the unique educational needs of visually impaired students and the roles and responsibilities of the personnel being supervised so that he or she may assist in improving the instruction and services being provided to meet these needs
- Is knowledgeable about the other areas outlined in this chapter, as well as funding sources (see Appendix B) and legal requirements (see Appendix G), so that he or she can be responsive and supportive of improving instruction and services based on the changing needs of students, staff, and parents.

Site administrator or designee
The site administrator or designee has the following roles and responsibilities:

- Is knowledgeable about the needs of visually impaired students and the roles and responsibilities of the regular teacher, the teacher of visually impaired students, and other staff working with these students
- Assists in the coordination of all instruction and services in the school, including regular course of study and special services (such as bilingual education and special education) and the implementation of alternative instructional strategies and proficiency standards
- Assists in promoting and supporting the appropriate placement of visually impaired students in the least

restrictive environment by facilitating the school's acceptance of the students, special staff, and the parents of the students as part of the school. (This acceptance can be supported through coordinated staff in-service training and parent education and the provision of information to all students in the school about visual impairments through classroom activities, cross-age tutoring, and student assemblies.)

- Provides facilities that are appropriate to meeting the unique needs of visually impaired students, as outlined later in this chapter.

PLACEMENT IN THE LEAST RESTRICTIVE ENVIRONMENT

STANDARD: Each visually impaired student is appropriately placed in the least restrictive environment on the basis of his or her educational needs.

When making decisions about placements, the individualized education program (IEP) team should (1) focus on the assessed educational needs and strengths of each visually impaired student, (2) determine a placement in which these needs can appropriately be met, and (3) change the placement as the needs of the student change.

The least restrictive environment as defined in P.L. 94-142 may vary for each student with the intensity of the student's needs, but specialized services that attend to the unique needs resulting from the student's visual impairment should also be provided. Students with needs that require intensive specialized instruction and services should be placed where these can be provided. Placing a student in an integrated setting where he or she does not have the skills or the necessary services to achieve and adapt in this setting can actually be more restrictive to the student. However, visually impaired students who have the necessary skills and services should be placed with nondisabled students to the maximum extent appropriate. But placement in an integrated setting does not mean the student is automatically integrated into the environment. It is important to prepare him or her for integration. Sighted peers and staff should also be prepared so that they have the knowledge, skills, and attitudes necessary to assist them in accepting the student without prejudice.

Often, an ideal placement where all a student's needs can be met at once does not exist. In such cases, the IEP team should look at the student's entire educational career, including possible future program options that can be expected to meet these needs better.

It is frequently appropriate to group visually impaired students who have additional disabilities with other students with similar needs, but specialized services that attend to the unique needs resulting from the student's visual impairment should also be provided. Students with a visual impairment as their sole or major disability should be grouped with nondisabled peers so that they can learn appropriate academic and behavioral models and appropriate levels of expectation for achievement.

In making the important placement decision, the IEP team should be creative, particularly in rural areas, in deciding on the option that will best meet the needs of each visually impaired student. Included in this process would be exploring regional programs, adapting existing programs, and investigating services provided by public and private agencies.

Program options

The following discussion outlines the recommended minimum options in a range of specialized services and programs available to visually impaired students. The various options are listed according to the intensity of instruction and services provided by the teacher of visually impaired students, from least intensive to most intensive.

The models described are identified by nationally accepted terminology rather than by funding terminology, because programs may be funded in a variety of ways, depending on local needs. Appendix B provides information about funding sources for the program options described.

Itinerant teacher. In the itinerant teacher model, students are enrolled in a regular classroom in the school they would attend if they were not visually impaired. Instruction is provided by a teacher of visually impaired children who visits students in their schools according to their needs for specialized services and also provides consultant services to staff and parents. (For additional discussion of the roles and responsibilities of this teacher, see Chapter Four.) If students have multiple disabilities and require specialized instruction to meet their unique educational needs, they are enrolled in various types of educational placements or special education classes. For children below school age, the itinerant teacher will provide intervention strategies by visiting the home or preschool setting.

Resource room. In the resource room model, students are placed in a special classroom for visually impaired youngsters who have more intensive needs that, ordinarily, require daily support services and specialized instruction provided by a teacher of visually impaired children. Students are integrated into regular and special education classrooms from the resource room for varying amounts of the school day based on their individual needs, as determined by the teacher of visually impaired children and the classroom teachers.

Self-contained classroom. In the self-contained classroom model, students are enrolled in a classroom for visually impaired students and ordinarily require specialized instruction for all or most of the school day. Instruction that emphasizes both subject matter skills and the development of special skills is provided by a teacher of visually impaired students in coordination with other appropriate staff. Students may profit by participating in regular classes in selected academic subjects or nonacademic areas as appropriate.

Special school. Students may also be enrolled in a special school that exclusively serves visually impaired students, including those with additional disabilities or unique needs. These students have the most intensive needs that require specialized instruction and support services beyond those that can reasonably or generally be provided in local school programs. Special school programs may be offered on a day or residential basis. These programs include the following:

- A special school in a local educational agency
- Residential schools for blind students (see Appendix E for a discussion of the role of residential schools)
- State hospital, developmental center, and intermediate care facility programs for visually impaired students (state Departments of Education listed in Appendix C can provide specific listings and relevant legal requirements).

Students enrolled in special school programs should have access to programs in local schools so that they are provided opportunities for integration as appropriate.

Nonpublic schools and agencies. A nonpublic school may be an educational option when a student's needs cannot be met by a public agency. Services may be provided by nonpublic schools and agencies when such services are not otherwise available, for example, orientation and mobility (O&M) instruction, instruction in daily living skills, and infant and preschool services.

Program options for infants and preschool children
Various options exist at the infant and preschool program level throughout the country. All program options may not be available in each state or community. The following options are cited as examples, not as a complete list:

- Public school programs for infants and preschool disabled children
- Nursery schools that are supported by parents, private organizations, adult education centers, and others
- Public and private home-based programs
- State preschool programs
- Children's centers, migrant child care centers, and campus children's centers
- School-age parenting and infant development programs
- Head Start programs
- Family counseling services, such as those that provide information and assistance to parents regarding their child's cognitive, physical, social, and emotional development; refer children to appropriate educational facilities; and assist infant and preschool teachers in methods of integrating and educating young visually impaired children.

A state's Department of Education can provide the location of programs offering counseling services and educational guidance to visually impaired infants and preschoolers and their families.

Parents should be provided with opportunities to meet with other parents of visually impaired children to exchange ideas and information and also to meet and consult with visually impaired adolescents and adults. Information about programs should be disseminated to parents through agencies and individuals involved in the identification and provision of services for visually impaired children. (See Appendix A for sources of information and Appendix H for information on legislation regarding services for infants and preschool children.)

CLASS SIZES AND CASELOADS
STANDARD: Class sizes and caseloads of staff allow for the provision of specialized instruction and services, based on the educational needs of visually impaired students.

It is essential to establish sizes of classes or caseloads for the teacher of visually impaired students and for the O&M specialist that are appropriate for the provision of instruction and services necessary to meet the unique educational needs of students with visual impairments. States may have legal requirements concerning caseload and class sizes. A state's Department of Education can indicate if requirements exist and, if so, what they are. In states that do not have legal requirements in this area, it is recommended that programs use one or both of the following approaches in determining class sizes and caseloads:

1. Establish and monitor the class size or caseload of the teacher of visually impaired students or O&M specialist on the basis of the time required for providing instruction based on the severity or intensity of students' needs; consulting with the classroom teacher and other staff, including consultation when a student is not receiving direct instruction; consulting with and assisting parents; traveling to carry out necessary responsibilities; securing and preparing needed specialized materials, media, and equipment; and attending meetings, preparing reports, and recordkeeping. Ongoing communication between the staff member and the responsible supervisor or administrator should be included in this process to ensure that students are receiving appropriate instruction and services in accordance with their IEPs and their changing needs.
2. Establish class sizes and caseloads based on the ages of the students being served and the severity of their needs and the instruction and services needed to meet those needs.

Table 1 shows ranges for class sizes and caseloads that are based on state and national averages for agencies. These ranges can be used as a general guide in establishing caseloads and class sizes on the local level. Local caseloads and class sizes for staff may fall above or below these ranges, according to the time requirements necessary for the teacher of visually impaired students and O&M specialist to complete the tasks just outlined.

STAFF AND SUPERVISION

STANDARD: A program provides qualified staff who have the skills and abilities to conduct assessments and to deliver instruction and services that meet the educational needs of visually impaired students.

The use of necessary qualified staff is a critical component in providing appropriate assessments, instruction, and services. Programs may use a range of qualified professionals.

Professional staff

Programs for visually impaired students should include the necessary appropriately credentialed or licensed professional staff, including the following (see Appendix G for legal requirements):

- Teachers of visually impaired students, who are certified in this area and possess the skills and abilities necessary to meet the unique educational needs of the students they serve, including state certification and/or certification from the Association for Education and Rehabilitation of the Blind and Visually Impaired (AER). (See Appendix A.)
- O&M specialists who are graduates of accredited college or university programs in this area and possess the skills and abilities necessary to meet the unique O&M needs of the visually impaired students they serve. O&M personnel may be certified by the state and/or AER.
- Assessment personnel, including a psychologist, as appropriate, who are knowledgeable about evaluating the needs and abilities of visually impaired students. (See Chapter Three for additional information regarding assessment personnel.)
- Other professional staff, including, but not limited to, regular and special education teachers; program specialists; language, speech, and hearing specialists; physical and occupational therapists; adapted phys-

Table 1. Average Ranges for Sizes of Classes and Caseloads

Type of program	Class size and caseload ranges
Resource room (one teacher and one aide)	8 to 12 students
Self-contained classroom (one teacher and one aide):	
For infants or preschool-age children	4 to 8 students
For kindergarten through third-grade children	6 to 10 students
For fourth- through twelfth-grade children	8 to 12 students
For children with multiple disabilities	3 to 7 students
Itinerant teacher	8 to 12 students
Orientation and mobility specialist	8 to 12 students
Home-based program for infants or preschool-age children	13 to 17 students

ical education specialists; school nurses; recreation therapists; social workers; and guidance counselors.

All staff should be knowledgeable about their roles and responsibilities in providing and coordinating needed instruction and services as outlined in Chapter Four. Personnel serving preschool children should have competencies and experience in the areas of education for visually impaired students and early childhood education.

Additional support staff
Each program for visually impaired students should also provide, as needed, transcribers, readers, aides, and other personnel who possess the skills necessary to meet unique educational needs.

STAFF DEVELOPMENT AND PARENT EDUCATION
STANDARD: Appropriate staff development and parental education are provided, based on a needs assessment that reflects the unique educational needs of visually impaired students.

Staff development based on continuing needs assessments should be provided for all special and regular education personnel. Efforts in this area should reflect the unique educational needs of visually impaired students and the roles and responsibilities of staff in meeting these needs. (See Chapter Four for a discussion of the roles and responsibilities of staff and Appendix G for legal requirements.)

Parent education based on a continuing needs assessment should be provided in every program for visually impaired students. It should emphasize the following two areas:

* Assisting parents in their roles and responsibilities of meeting the special developmental needs of their visually impaired children through ongoing communication (see Chapter Four for a discussion of the roles and responsibilities of parents)
* Providing parents with needed information pertinent to the education of their children, including information regarding the range of educational programs and related agencies and services at local, state, regional, and national levels.

GUIDELINES FOR FACILITIES
STANDARD: Facilities are designed or modified to enhance the provision of instruction and services to meet the unique educational needs of visually impaired students.

Facilities should be provided to meet the unique educational needs of visually impaired students. Resource rooms or self-contained classrooms used for these students should be the standard size of regular classrooms in the school system and should include:

* Appropriate and adjustable lighting that meets or surpasses minimum standards and satisfies the needs of low vision students
* Adequate storage space for special equipment
* A separate area for listening activities
* Furniture and chalkboards (black or green) with nonglare surfaces
* A sufficient number of electrical outlets for specialized equipment
* A location on the site that provides convenient accessibility for all visually impaired students attending regular classes.

The teacher of visually impaired students should provide assistance in designing and modifying facilities to meet the needs of students who will be using them. The following guidelines should be considered:

* Appropriate bathroom facilities should be provided for students with multiple disabilities and students in primary school
* Adequate working space with proper lighting for individual instruction and counseling should be available in each school attended by a visually impaired student and served by an itinerant teacher
* Adequate space should be provided in regular classrooms for the visually impaired student's specialized equipment and materials
* Office space should be available for itinerant teachers and O&M instructors. This space should include adequate storage areas, telephones, an answering service, and clerical assistance.

Adequate working space for transcribers should be provided. Special equipment should be available as needed for the production and duplication of materials, including large-print typewriters and duplicators, tape recording equipment and duplicators, braillewriters, and braille duplicating equipment.

Programs for visually impaired preschool children should be housed in a school or facility in which the following modifications have been made:

* Other preschool programs are available for nondisabled children to provide integration opportunities for visually impaired children

- Bathroom facilities have been designed or adapted for young children
- Playground facilities are adjacent to the classroom and include space for appropriate toys and equipment.

In addition, students with visual impairments, like all other students, should receive instruction and practice in responding appropriately and calmly to emergencies by participating in fire, tornado, and earthquake drills, bus evacuation drills, and other emergency procedures. The specialized health care needs of these students, such as those with high-risk medical conditions involving the possible onset of diabetic shock or seizure disorders, must be taken into account when emergency procedures are planned. Local codes and ordinances regarding such procedures should be followed.

Staff should be prepared to handle emergencies and should have a knowledge of the specific procedures to follow. The teacher of visually impaired students or the O&M specialist should provide assistance to students and staff regarding evacuation routes and procedures. The school nurse should assist with procedures to follow for medical emergencies.

MATERIALS AND EQUIPMENT

STANDARD: Materials and equipment necessary to meet the unique educational needs of visually impaired students are provided, as indicated by the students' IEPs.

Materials and equipment must be provided as indicated in the IEP of each visually impaired student to meet the unique educational needs of the student. (See Appendix G for legal requirements.) Sufficient time must also be allocated for the transcriber or teacher of visually impaired students to locate, prepare, and disseminate materials and equipment for each student.

Because expensive materials and equipment are often not available from other sources, funds at the local level must be budgeted to ensure that necessary books, materials, and equipment are provided, coordinated, and maintained. Specialized books, materials, and equipment indicated in the IEPs of visually impaired students must be provided.

Materials and equipment purchased with federal or state funds by local educational agencies may remain the property of the state and be reassigned when they are no longer being used locally. (See Appendix B for sources of funding and Appendix G for legal requirements.) An organized, cost-effective, and coordinated system for acquiring, coordinating, disseminating, and maintaining these special materials and equipment should be operated from central locations within the state, region, or district by specific individuals assigned this responsibility.

TRANSPORTATION

STANDARD: Transportation for visually impaired students is suitable to the unique health and safety needs of these students.

When visually impaired students are transported to special classes or schools, specific arrangements need to be made. They include the following:

- Transportation arranged is appropriate to the health and safety of the students, including consideration of the travel time involved
- Through continuing in-service training by the O&M instructor or teacher of visually impaired students, drivers are made aware of unique O&M needs and measures that may be useful, including emergency, drop-off, and pick-up procedures
- Students are encouraged to travel independently to and from school when they have the necessary O&M skills.

PROGRAM IMPROVEMENT

STANDARD: A program serving visually impaired students has an ongoing process to evaluate its effectiveness and improve the identification and assessment of needs and the planning and provision of instruction and services in meeting the unique educational needs of these students.

Each program serving visually impaired students should have an ongoing process for evaluating its effectiveness in meeting students' needs and using the evaluation results in program improvement. The evaluation process should encompass all the areas outlined in this book, using the standards discussed in each chapter and the "Self-Review Guide" presented in Chapter Six as the basis for the review.

When conducting a self-review, program planners should develop specific questions for interviewing administrators, special and regular education staff, and parents and for reviewing students' records and other documentation. Interview questions should be open-ended and begin with formulations such as "how," "what," "who," and "when," as appropriate. This approach will provide more valuable information for determining and improving the effectiveness of a program than will simple "yes" or "no" questions. The approach can also clarify who is responsible for the elements of the program and yield a local consensus for possible evaluation studies on the local level.

The guidelines outlined in these chapters should be considered when programs serving visually impaired students are monitored by a state Department of Education. The department also should provide technical assistance to parents, teachers, and administrators in the implementation of these guidelines. (See Appendix E for discussion of the role of the state education consultant; other sources of information can be found in the "Selected Reading List.")

CHAPTER SIX

Self-review guide

This self-review guide contains criteria for evaluating the components of educational programs that were outlined in Chapters Three through Five. The criteria correspond to the specific standards and guidelines in these chapters.

To rate the level of effectiveness of a program, reviewers should check beside each criterion one of the numbers shown under the column heading "Program Effectiveness." The ratings that the numbers represent are shown at the bottom of the table. Information in the text that relates to the criteria can be located by referring to the page or chapter numbers or appendixes given in the "Reference" column.

CHAPTER THREE—IDENTIFYING AND ASSESSING UNIQUE EDUCATIONAL NEEDS

Reference	Criteria	Program effectiveness[1]				Comments
		1	2	3	4	
	How effective is your program in providing for each of the following:					
p. 15 Appendix G	I. *Locating and referring students with visual impairments who may require special education, including possible referrals from vision screening programs?*					
p. 15	A. Providing the process for referring students identified through vision screening?					
p. 15	B. Informing parents and staff of signs that may indicate a visual impairment?					
p. 15	C. Coordinating with local eye specialists and other referral sources?					
p. 15	II. *Assessing students with suspected visual impairments in all of the following areas where appropriate?*					
p. 15 Appendix D	A. Assessing vision/low vision:					
	1. Acquiring as much information as possible on eye reports?					
	2. Ensuring that students with low vision receive a low vision assessment?					
	a. Conducting functional vision assessments?					
	b. Determining the need for further assessment?					
	c. Using the low vision assessment to determine needs in the other areas related to this disability?					

[1]Program effectiveness: 1=ineffective, 2=somewhat effective, 3=effective, 4=very effective.

(Continued on next page)

Identifying and Assessing Unique Educational Needs *(Continued)*

Reference	Criteria	Program effectiveness[1]				Comments
		1	2	3	4	
p. 16	B. Assessing concept development and academic skills:					
	1. Coordinating with the classroom teacher?					
	2. Determining the students' mode of functioning in academic tasks?					
	3. Developing basic concepts?					
	4. Listening skills?					
	5. Study skills?					
p. 17	C. Assessing communication skills:					
	1. Typing?					
	2. Signature?					
	3. Familiarity with communication equipment?					
	4. Use of computers?					
	5. Use of optical aids?					
	6. Closed-circuit televisions?					
	7. Braille/slate and stylus and brailler?					
	8. Abacus?					
	9. Talking calculators?					
	10. Use of specialized equipment?					
p. 17	D. Assessing social/emotional skills:					
	1. Socialization skills?					
	2. Affective education?					
	3. Recreation?					
	4. Human sexuality?					
	5. Psychological implications of the visual impairment?					
p. 17	E. Assessing sensory/motor skills:					
	1. Gross and fine motor skills?					
	2. Alternative sensory discrimination and integration skills?					
	3. Posture, balance, strength, movement, and coordination?					
p. 17	F. Assessing orientation and mobility skills:					
	1. Concepts?					
	2. Body image, control, and purposeful movement?					
	3. Orientation and mobility skills?					
	a. At home?					

[1]Program effectiveness: 1=ineffective, 2=somewhat effective, 3=effective, 4=very effective.

(Continued on next page)

Reference	Criteria	Program effectiveness[1]				Comments
		1	2	3	4	
	b. School?					
	c. Community?					
	4. Use of vision?					
	5. Interaction with the public?					
	6. Acquiring and remembering necessary information?					
	7. Related daily living skills?					
p.17	G. Assessing daily living skills:					
	1. Personal hygiene?					
	2. Dressing skills?					
	3. Clothing care?					
	4. Housekeeping skills?					
	5. Food preparation?					
	6. Eating skills?					
	7. Money management?					
	8. Social communication?					
	9. Telephone skills?					
	10. Written communication?					
	11. Time skills?					
	12. Organization skills?					
p. 18	H. Assessing career and vocational skills:					
	1. Awareness?					
	2. Exploration?					
	3. Preparation?					
	4. Participation?					
p. 18 Appendix G	III. *Providing assessment personnel who are knowledgeable about visual impairments:*					
p. 18	A. Providing for communication among individuals conducting assessments?					
p. 18	B. Involving the teacher of visually impaired students in determining appropriate assessment strategies?					
p. 18	C. Determining the best qualified individual to conduct assessments?					
p. 18 Appendix G	IV. *Identifying in the assessment report the student's unique educational needs related to the visual impairment, including needs for specialized materials and equipment in the following areas:*					
	A. Vision/low vision needs?					
	B. Concept development and academic needs?					

[1]Program effectiveness: 1=ineffective, 2=somewhat effective, 3=effective, 4=very effective.

(Continued on next page)

Reference	Criteria	Program effectiveness[1]				Comments
		1	2	3	4	
	C. Communication needs?					
	D. Social/emotional needs?					
	E. Sensory/motor needs?					
	F. Orientation and mobility needs?					
	G. Daily living skills needs?					
	H. Career and vocational needs?					
p. 18 Appendix G	V. *Considering the variables that affect unique educational needs when the following are assessed:*					
p. 19	A. Congenitally and adventitiously visually impaired students?					
p. 19	B. Students with multiple impairments?					
p. 19	C. Infants and preschool children?					
p. 19	D. Elementary and secondary students?					
p. 20	E. The nature of the visual impairment?					
p. 20	F. Functionally blind and low vision students?					
p. 20	G. Students with other special needs?					

CHAPTER FOUR—PLANNING AND PROVIDING INSTRUCTION AND SERVICES

Reference	Criteria	Program effectiveness[1]				Comments
		1	2	3	4	
	How effective is your program in providing for each of the following:					
p. 21 Appendix G	VI. *Using assessed unique educational needs in the following areas?*					
p. 21	A. Developing the IEP, including the need for specialized materials and equipment in the following areas:					
	1. Concept development and academic needs?					
	2. Communication needs?					
	3. Social/emotional needs?					
	4. Sensory/motor needs?					
	5. Orientation and mobility needs?					
	6. Daily living skills needs?					
	7. Career and vocational needs?					

[1]Program effectiveness: 1=ineffective, 2=somewhat effective, 3=effective, 4=very effective.

(Continued on next page)

Reference	Criteria	Program effectiveness[1]				Comments
		1	2	3	4	
p. 21	B. Providing appropriate instruction and services in the following areas:					
	1. Concept development and academic needs?					
	2. Communication needs?					
	3. Social/emotional needs?					
	4. Sensory/motor needs?					
	5. Orientation and mobility needs?					
	6. Daily living skills needs?					
	7. Career and vocational needs?					
p. 21	C. Developing curriculum:					
	1. Concept development and academic needs?					
	2. Communication needs?					
	3. Social/emotional needs?					
	4. Sensory/motor needs?					
	5. Orientation and mobility needs?					
	6. Daily living skills needs?					
	7. Career and vocational needs?					
p. 25	D. Providing the necessary equipment and materials in accordance with the IEP to meet the unique educational needs for:					
	1. Functionally blind students?					
	2. Low vision students?					
	3. Multiply impaired students?					
	4. Nonacademic students, infants, and preschool children?					
p. 25 Appendix G	VII. *Ensuring that the following key individuals understand the unique needs of visually impaired students and possess the skills and abilities to carry out their roles and responsibilities:*					
p. 25	A. Teacher of visually impaired students?					
p. 26	B. Classroom teacher (regular, special class, or resource specialist)?					
p. 26	C. Orientation and mobility specialist?					
p. 27	D. Parent, guardian, or conservator?					
p. 28	E. Visually impaired student?					
p. 28	F. Eye specialist?					

[1]Program effectiveness: 1=ineffective, 2=somewhat effective, 3=effective, 4=very effective.

(Continued on next page)

Reference	Criteria	Program effectiveness[1]				Comments
		1	2	3	4	
p. 28	G. Regular or adapted physical education specialist?					
p. 28	H. Occupational or physical therapist?					
p. 28	I. School nurse?					
p. 28	J. Program specialist?					
p. 29	K. Specialist in career and vocational education?					
p. 29	L. Language, speech, and hearing specialist?					
p. 29	M. Counselor, psychologist, or social worker?					
p. 29	N. Transcriber/recorder?					
p. 29	O. Reader?					
p. 29	P. Aide?					

p. 29	Q. Ancillary staff in residential programs:
	  1. Dormitory or other residential care personnel?
	  2. Food services staff?
	  3. Health services staff?					

p. 30	VIII. *Coordinating the instruction and services provided to meet all of the needs of visually impaired students:*					
p. 30	A. Using the IEP as the focus for coordination?					
p. 30	B. Assigning an individual responsible for this coordination?					

CHAPTER FIVE—ORGANIZING AND SUPPORTING INSTRUCTION AND SERVICES

Reference	Criteria	Program effectiveness[1]				Comments
		1	2	3	4	
	How effective is your program in providing for each of the following:					
p. 31 Appendix G	IX. *Providing for the delivery of appropriate instruction and services through a full range*					

[1]Program effectiveness: 1=ineffective, 2=somewhat effective, 3=effective, 4=very effective.

(Continued on next page)

Reference	Criteria	Program effectiveness[1]				Comments
		1	2	3	4	
	of program options that are established, as necessary, on a regional basis:					
p. 31	A. Providing necessary instruction and services through regionalization?					
p. 31	B. Ensuring that administrative roles and responsibilities are understood by:					
	1. Regional special education agencies?					
	2. The supervisor of personnel serving visually impaired students?					
	3. The site administrator or designee?					
p. 32 Appendix G	X. *Placing students appropriately in the least restrictive environment:*					
p. 32	A. Considering the changing needs and strengths of students?					
p. 32	B. Placing students based on the intensity of needs and the intensity of instructional services to meet these needs?					
p. 32	C. Preparing the student for integration?					
p. 32	D. Preparing school staff and peers for integration?					
p. 32	E. Grouping students appropriately?					
p. 32	F. Exploring additional program options?					
p. 32	G. Providing the following program options, when needed, through regionalization:					
	1. Itinerant teacher?					
	2. Resource room?					
	3. Self-contained classroom?					
	4. Special school?					
	5. Nonpublic schools and agencies?					
	6. Additional options for infants and preschool children?					
p. 33	XI. *Establishing class sizes and caseloads of staff to allow for providing specialized instruction and services based on the educational needs of visually impaired students by:*					
p. 34	A. Developing a process for establishing and monitoring class sizes and caseloads based on the time required to meet students' needs?					

[1]Program effectiveness: 1=ineffective, 2=somewhat effective, 3=effective, 4=very effective.

(Continued on next page)

Reference	Criteria	Program effectiveness[1]				Comments
		1	2	3	4	
p. 34	B. Establishing local caseloads and class sizes based on the ages of the students and the severity of their needs?					
p. 34	XII. *Providing qualified professional and paraprofessional personnel who have the skills and abilities necessary to conduct assessments and deliver instruction and services that meet the educational needs of students:*					
p. 34	A. Professional staff:					
	1. Appropriately credentialed teachers of visually impaired students?					
	2. Appropriately credentialed orientation and mobility specialists?					
	3. Assessment personnel?					
	4. Other professional staff as needed?					
p. 35	B. Additional support staff:					
	1. Transcribers?					
	2. Readers?					
	3. Aides?					
	4. Other staff as needed?					
p. 35 Appendix G	XIII. *Providing staff development and education for parents based on a needs assessment:*					
p. 35	A. Basing the needs assessment for parent education on parents' roles and responsibilities and the unique educational needs of their children?					
p. 35	B. Basing the needs assessment for staff development on the staff members' roles and responsibilities and the unique educational needs of the students they serve?					
p. 35	XIV. *Designing and modifying facilities to enhance the provision of instruction and services to meet the unique educational needs of visually impaired students in the following areas:*					
p. 35	A. Facilities for school-age students:					
	1. Lighting?					
	2. Equipment, storage space, and electrical outlets?					
	3. An area for listening activities?					

[1]Program effectiveness: 1=ineffective, 2=somewhat effective, 3=effective, 4=very effective.

(Continued on next page)

Organizing and Supporting Instruction and Services *(Continued)*

Reference	Criteria	Program effectiveness[1]				Comments
		1	2	3	4	
	4. Furniture with nonglare surfaces?					
	5. Accessibility?					
	6. Bathroom facilities?					
	7. Work area for students being served by an intinerant teacher?					
	8. Work space for the transcriber?					
	9. Special equipment for production and duplication of materials?					
p. 35	B. Facilities for infants and preschool children:					
	1. Opportunities for integration with nondisabled students?					
	2. Bathroom facilities?					
	3. Playground and storage space?					
p. 36	C. Emergency procedures?					
p. 36 Appendix G	XV. *Providing curriculum materials in special media (braille, large print, tape) and other educational materials and equipment necessary to meet the unique educational needs of students, as specified in the IEP:*					
p. 36	A. Allowing time for the teacher or transcriber, or both, to locate, prepare, and disseminate materials and equipment?					
p. 36	B. Establishing a system for budgeting that projects costs of equipment and materials?					
p. 36	C. Establishing an organized, cost-effective, and coordinated system for acquiring, disseminating, and maintaining specialized equipment and materials?					
p. 36 Appendix G	XVI. *Providing appropriate transportation for visually impaired students by:*					
p. 36	A. Considering health and safety, including travel time?					
p. 36	B. Providing continuing in-service training to drivers?					
p. 36	C. Encouraging students to travel independently when appropriate?					
p. 36 Appendix G	XVII. *Establishing a process to improve the effectiveness of programs in meeting the needs of visually impaired students in these areas:*					

[1]Program effectiveness: 1=ineffective, 2=somewhat effective, 3=effective, 4=very effective.

(Continued on next page)

Organizing and Supporting Instruction and Services *(Continued)*

Reference	Criteria	Program effectiveness[1]				Comments
		1	2	3	4	
Ch. Three	A. Identification?					
Ch. Three	B. Assessment?					
Ch. Four	C. Planning?					
Ch. Four and Five	D. Providing instruction and services?					
p. 36	E. Using the information obtained through a self-review process to:					
	1. Identify areas of need and suggestions for improvement?					
	2. Identify areas of strength?					
	3. Identify needs for technical assistance?					
	4. Coordinate with monitoring activities of the state Department of Education?					
	5. Identify possible topics for local evaluation studies?					

[1]Program effectiveness: 1=ineffective, 2=somewhat effective, 3=effective, 4=very effective.

Appendixes

Selected Readings

Glossary

Resources for technical assistance

A state's Department of Education can provide information on special education programs and answer questions on such matters as identification, assessment, instruction and services, curriculum, public school programs and private schools and agencies, and funding and legal requirements. It can also supply information about rehabilitation agencies and services, orientation and mobility services, teacher preparation programs, certification requirements, state hospitals/developmental centers, low vision services, vocational education, vision screening, and related services for students with special needs. (See Appendix C for state Department of Education listings.)

OTHER SOURCES OF INFORMATION

Information about residential programs, including summer school programs and diagnostic centers, can be obtained from a state's residential school for blind and visually impaired students. The state Department of Education can identify the nearest public or private residential school. Information about materials and equipment, aural media, and transcribers is available through the state's instructional materials center, depository, or clearinghouse. Every state does not have an instructional materials center. The state Department of Education should be able to identify the nearest center for special media and materials provided for blind and visually impaired students. (Appendix B outlines sources of equipment and materials.) Additional information on dog guide schools, other services, and programs in other states is available from the American Foundation for the Blind, whose address and telephone number are listed under "Additional Resources" in this appendix.

ADDITIONAL RESOURCES

American Foundation for the Blind
15 West 16th Street
New York, NY 10011
(212) 620-2000 or (800) 232-5463

The American Foundation for the Blind (AFB) provides direct and technical assistance services to blind and visually impaired persons and their families, professionals, and organizations and agencies. AFB acts as a national clearinghouse for information about blindness and visual impairment and operates a toll-free national hotline. It has a scholarship program and provides catalogs of publications, media, and devices and appliances. The services of national and regional consultants and a variety of publications, including the *Directory of Services for Blind and Visually Impaired Persons in the United States*, 23rd Edition, are also available from AFB. In addition, AFB operates the following regional centers:

Mid-Atlantic Regional Center
1615 M Street, N.W., Suite 250
Washington, DC 20036
(202) 457-1487

Serves Delaware, District of Columbia, Kentucky, Maryland, Ohio, Pennsylvania, Virginia, and West Virginia.

Midwest Regional Center
20 North Wacker Drive, Suite 1938
Chicago, IL 60606
(312) 269-0095

Serves Illinois, Indiana, Iowa, Michigan, Minnesota, Missouri, and Wisconsin.

Northeast Regional Center
15 West 16th Street
New York, NY 10011
(212) 620-2003

Serves Connecticut, Maine, Massachusetts, New Hampshire, New Jersey, New York, Rhode Island, and Vermont.

Southeast Regional Center
100 Peachtree Street, Suite 680
Atlanta, GA 30303
(404) 525-2303

Serves Alabama, Arkansas, Florida, Georgia, Louisiana, Mississippi, North Carolina, Puerto Rico, South Carolina, Tennessee, and the Virgin Islands.

Southwest Regional Center
260 Treadway Plaza
Exchange Park
Dallas, TX 75235
(214) 352-7222

Serves Colorado, Kansas, Montana, Nebraska, New Mexico, North Dakota, Oklahoma, South Dakota, Texas, and Wyoming.

Western Regional Center
111 Pine Street, Suite 725
San Francisco, CA 94111
(415) 392-4845

Serves Alaska, Arizona, California, Guam, Hawaii, Idaho, Nevada, Oregon, Utah, and Washington.

Association for Education and Rehabilitation of the Blind and Visually Impaired
206 North Washington Street, Suite 320
Alexandria, VA 22314
(703) 548-1884

The Association for Education and Rehabilitation of the Blind and Visually Impaired (AER) is a membership organization dedicated to the education and rehabilitation of blind and visually impaired children and adults. The organization and its chapters conduct local, regional, and international meetings and conferences; provide continuing education programs and publications, including newsletters and a journal; and operate a job exchange and reference information service. AER contains several special interest groups in such areas as early childhood, elementary education, and orientation and mobility. The addresses of local chapters can be obtained from AER's national headquarters.

Council for Exceptional Children
1920 Association Drive
Reston, VA 22091
(703) 620-3660

The Council for Exceptional Children (CEC) publishes a magazine, newsletters, and position papers and hosts national meetings. CEC provides information to teachers, parents, and professionals. It has a Division for the Visually Handicapped.

National Association for Parents of the Visually Impaired
P.O. Box 562
Camden, NY 13316
(315) 245-3442, 245-3444 or (800) 562-6265

The National Association for Parents of the Visually Impaired (NAPVI) holds national and chapter conferences and provides peer support, information, and services to parents and families of visually impaired and multiply impaired students. The addresses of local chapters can be obtained from NAPVI's national headquarters.

American Council of the Blind
1010 Vermont Avenue, N.W., Suite 1100
Washington, DC 20005
(202) 393-3666

National Federation of the Blind
1800 Johnson Street
Baltimore, MD 21230
(301) 659-9314

The American Council of the Blind (ACB) and the National Federation of the Blind (NFB) are organizations of blind persons and can provide assistance to school staff and parents. Both organizations have parent groups and scholarship programs. ACB provides information and referrals, legal assistance, advocacy support, and a variety of consultative and advisory services. NFB operates a public education program, provides evaluation of existing programs and assistance in establishing new ones, and has a network of state affiliates. The addresses of affiliates can be obtained from NFB's national headquarters.

National Association for Visually Handicapped
22 West 21st Street
New York, NY 10010
(212) 889-3141

National Society to Prevent Blindness
500 East Remington Road
Schaumburg, IL 60173
(312) 843-2020

The National Association for Visually Handicapped (NAVH) and the National Society to Prevent Blindness (NSPB) work to prevent blindness and eye injury through public awareness programs. NAVH provides large-type reading materials, acts as an information clearinghouse and referral center, and sells low vision devices. NSPB conducts a program of public and professional education, research, and industrial and community services and has a network of state affiliates. The addresses can be obtained from NSPB's national headquarters.

American Council on Rural Special Education
National Rural Development Institute

Western Washington University
Miller Hall 359
Bellingham, WA 98225
(206) 676-3576

The American Council on Rural Special Education (ACRES) specializes in services for exceptional students and their families residing in rural areas. ACRES distributes information, advocates for services, and conducts task forces on rural problems and issues.

Association for Persons with Severe Handicaps
7010 Roosevelt Way, N.E.
Seattle, WA 98115
(206) 523-8446

The Association for Persons with Severe Handicaps (TASH) advocates for educational services for persons with disabilities. TASH disseminates information, publishes a newsletter and a journal, and acts as an advocate for the rights of disabled persons.

Association for Retarded Citizens
2501 Avenue J
Arlington, TX 76006
(817) 640-0204

The Association for Retarded Citizens (ARC) works on local, state, and national levels to promote services, public understanding, and legislation for mentally retarded persons and their families.

American Association of the Deaf-Blind
c/o 814 Thayer Avenue
Silver Spring, MD 20910
(301) 588-6545

The American Association of the Deaf-Blind (AADB) is a consumer organization of deaf-blind persons. AADB is involved in advocacy activities and holds an annual convention for deaf-blind persons and their families to discuss critical issues regarding deaf-blindness.

Helen Keller National Center for Deaf-Blind Youths and Adults
111 Middle Neck Road
Sands Point, NY 11050
(516) 944-8900

The Helen Keller National Center for Deaf-Blind Youths and Adults provides services and technical assistance to deaf-blind individuals and maintains a network of regional and affiliate agencies. The addresses of affiliates can be obtained from the national headquarters office.

National Coalition for Deaf-Blindness
c/o Perkins School for the Blind
175 North Beacon Street
Watertown, MA 02172
(617) 924-3434

The National Coalition for Deaf-Blindness advocates in behalf of the interests of deaf-blind persons and provides information to consumers and professionals.

National Accreditation Council for Agencies Serving the Blind and Visually Handicapped
232 Madison Avenue, Suite 907
New York, NY 10016
(212) 779-8080

The National Accreditation Council (NAC) for Agencies Serving the Blind and Visually Handicapped is the primary certifying agency of facilities serving visually impaired individuals, including residential schools and low vision clinics. NAC formulates and updates standards for services and publishes them in various media.

National Association of State Directors of Special Education
2021 K Street, N.W., Suite 315
Washington, DC 20006
(202) 296-1800

The National Association of State Directors of Special Education (NASDE) provides assistance to state education agencies and offers consultative services. NASDE publishes newsletters and also sponsors conferences.

National Braille Association
1290 University Avenue
Rochester, NY 14607
(716) 473-0900

The National Braille Association is concerned with the production and distribution of braille, large-type, and tape-recorded materials for visually impaired people.

Office of Special Education and Rehabilitative Services
330 C Street, S.W., Room 3132
Washington, DC 20202
(202) 732-1241

The Office of Special Education and Rehabilitative Services (OSERS) has federal oversight responsibility for special education services.

Sources of funding and materials and equipment

The funding of program options for visually impaired students, such as those outlined in Chapter Five, varies from state to state. A state's Department of Education (see Appendix C) can be contacted for information on specific state legislation to fund the following: public school programs, state hospitals and developmental centers, state-supported residential schools, and private schools and agencies.

LOW VISION DEVICES
Nonprescriptive low vision devices may be funded by local and other public agencies. Additional funding sources, particularly for prescriptive low vision devices (which are not generally funded by the local educational agency), may be:
- the state agency for children's services (Department of Health)
- the state Department of Rehabilitation
- insurance coverage of the parent
- Medicaid
- regional centers
- service organizations, particularly local Lions International Clubs, whose major service interests have traditionally related to visually handicapped people, and Kiwanis International Clubs, whose major service interests have traditionally related to young people.

FUNDING FOR MATERIALS AND EQUIPMENT
Local education budgets must include sufficient funds for providing books, equipment, and materials for visually impaired students. Special state funding is usually available to purchase and coordinate the use of specialized equipment and materials for these students. Information about approximate equipment costs is provided in Table 1.

An additional source of funding for materials and equipment for legally blind students is the federal appropriation administered by the American Printing House (APH) for the Blind Federal Quota Program. At present, there are 161 organizations that are registering students for this program. Among them are state instructional materials centers, Departments of Education, and residential schools for blind and visually impaired students. Program staff should contact all potential

Table 1. Average Local Education Agency Costs for a Sample of Basic Materials and Equipment[a]

Braille materials (yearly per student)	$ 523
Large-print materials (yearly per student) .	520
Closed-circuit television system	2,600
Large-print typewriter	400
Magnifying devices	25–65
Orientation and mobility cane	20
Paperless brailler	6,000

[a]Figures shown are approximate and are based on 1985 estimates. Current costs may vary from the dollar amounts shown.

resources before purchasing new equipment and materials to ascertain their usefulness and cost-effectiveness. Finally, local service clubs and other community groups may help provide funds for equipment and materials when no other funding source is available.

SOURCES OF MATERIALS AND EQUIPMENT
Sources of materials and equipment are the state's instructional materials center and the Library of Congress National Library Service (NLS) for the Blind and Physically Handicapped. Additional sources may be available in various states, and a state's Department of Education may be contacted for additional information. (See Appendix C for state Department of Education listings and Appendix E for more information on instructional materials centers, which are also called instructional resource centers.)

Some states have formally organized delivery systems for specialized materials for blind and visually impaired students. These may be referred to as instructional materials centers (or instructional resource centers), clearinghouses, or depositories. The APH program (described in the following section of this appendix) represents one model for the delivery of materials; clearinghouses and depositories are additional models. Clearinghouses receive and process requests, arrange for shipment to the requester, and keep an inventory so that materials can be recirculated. Depositories provide the same services and, in addition, house used books and equipment. Many instructional materials centers, clearinghouses, and depositories offer other services, such as information dissemination, technical assistance, in-service training, materials production, and loan of materials not available through APH.

American Printing House for the Blind
Federal Quota Program

Each year Congress appropriates a specific sum of money to APH for use in developing and supplying books in special media as well as specialized devices and equipment for educating blind students in the nation. States may acquire materials and equipment from APH without cost up to the amount of their federal quota allocation.

As indicated earlier, the APH Federal Quota Program is administered by the state agency designated as responsible to do so (i.e., the state instructional materials center, Department of Education, or residential school). During January of each year, the responsible agency conducts registration of blind students in the state to establish the state's proportional credit allotment with APH. Although the allotment is made to the state, the allotment from the annual federal quota appropriation is apportioned on the basis of the number of blind students registered. Information on the specific procedures used in this process can be obtained from the specific agency. For additional information, the following address can be used:

American Printing House for the Blind
P.O. Box 6085
1839 Frankfort Avenue
Louisville, KY 40206
(502) 895-2405

National Library Service

Reading materials for blind and physically handicapped individuals are provided by the U.S. government through NLS and are made available through 54 regional branch libraries. Eligibility for this program encompasses all age groups, including preschoolers, and a broad range of visual and physical limitations that make reading standard printed materials difficult or impossible.

Braille books may be borrowed by any visually handicapped person on request to the regional libraries. Talking Books and cassette tapes may be borrowed by any person who has been certified as being unable to handle or read conventional print materials because of a visual or physical handicap and who has the proper equipment (also available through NLS) on which to play the records and tapes. Catalogs of braille books, records, and tapes are furnished so that the applicant can make selections. The regional libraries will select books, if requested, for those who do not care to make their own selections.

In addition to an extensive collection maintained for adults, a collection of books in braille and on Talking Book records is available for children. Also, many titles are available that are suitable for use by young adults, both for recreational reading and as reading required for courses of study.

The library service is free to blind and physically handicapped readers. Books are sent postage free to the borrower and are returned in the same manner. The lending period for materials is five weeks. Each braille volume, Talking Book, or tape container must be returned as soon as it has been finished. When that volume or container is received at the library, another one is sent in return. In this way, the reader always has something on hand to read.

Talking Book machines and cassette players are available on loan following the completion of an application processed through the reader's regional library and for as long as the reader uses the service. Local public librarians can provide additional information regarding the services available and the procedures to be followed. For further information, the following address can also be used:

Library of Congress National Library Service
for the Blind and Physically Handicapped
1291 Taylor Street, N.W.
Washington, DC 20542
(202) 287-5100 or (800) 424-9100

Other Sources of Equipment and Materials

Other sources of materials and equipment include the American Foundation for the Blind (AFB) and Recording for the Blind (RFB). A catalog of publications and a catalog of devices and equipment are available without charge from AFB. RFB is a major source of recorded textbooks for students from the fifth grade through college level (there is an initial fee for service). Books not already recorded may be recorded on request by a regional studio of RFB. (A catalog is available for a fee.) Readers in states in which there is no regional studio can contact the studio located nearest to them. Information on local studios can be obtained from RFB or from the *Directory of Services for Blind and Visually*

Impaired Persons in the United States, 23rd Edition (New York: American Foundation for the Blind, 1988). For additional information, the following addresses can be used:

American Foundation for the Blind
15 West 16th Street
New York, NY 10011
(212) 620-2000 or (800) 232-5463

Recording for the Blind
20 Roszel Road
Princeton, NJ 08540
(609) 452-0606

State departments of education

A state's Department of Education can provide essential information on educational services and programs in the state, including referrals to local special education administrators for information about local programs for visually impaired students. This appendix lists special education units/state Departments of Education in every state and in the District of Columbia, Guam, Puerto Rico, and the Virgin Islands.

Alabama State Department of Education
1020 Monticello Court
Montgomery, AL 36117
(205) 261-5099 or toll-free in Alabama
(800) 392-8020

Alaska Department of Education
Goldbelt Building
P.O. Box F
Juneau, AK 99811
(907) 465-2800

Arizona Department of Education
Division of Special Education
1535 West Jefferson
Phoenix, AZ 85007
(602) 255-3183

Arkansas Department of Education
Special Education
54 Capitol Mall
Education Building, Room 105-C
Little Rock, AR 72201
(501) 371-2161

California Department of Education
Special Education Division
721 Capitol Mall
P.O. Box 944272
Sacramento, CA 94244-2720
(916) 323-4768

Colorado Department of Education
Special Education Services Unit and
Colorado Instructional Materials Center for the
Visually Handicapped (CIMC/VH)

201 East Colfax Avenue
Denver, CO 80203
(303) 866-6694

Connecticut State Board of Education and
Services for the Blind
170 Ridge Road
Wethersfield, CT 06109
(203) 249-8525

Delaware Department of Public Instruction
John G. Townsend Building
P.O. Box 1402
Dover, DE 19903
(302) 736-5471

District of Columbia Division of Special Education
and Public Personnel Services
District of Columbia Public Schools
Webster Administration Building
10th Street and H Street, N.W.
Washington, DC 20001
(202) 724-4018

Florida Department of Education
Bureau of Education for Exceptional Students
Knott Building
Tallahassee, FL 32399-0400
(904) 488-1461

Georgia State Department of Education
Program for Exceptional Children
1970 Twin Towers East
Atlanta, GA 30334-5040
(404) 656-6317

Guam Department of Education
P.O. Box DE
Agana, GU 96910
011+(671) 472-8901

Hawaii Department of Education
Honolulu District Office

4697 Kilauea Avenue
Honolulu, HI 96816
(808) 737-5694

Idaho State Department of Education
650 West State Street
Boise, ID 83720
(208) 334-3940

Illinois State Board of Education
Department of Specialized Educational Services
100 North First Street
Springfield, IL 62777
(217) 782-6601

State of Indiana Department of Education
Division of Special Education
State House, Room 229
Indianapolis, IN 46204
(317) 269-9462

Iowa Department of Education
Grimes State Office Building
Des Moines, IA 50319-0146
(515) 281-5294

Kansas Division of Special Education
120 East Tenth Street
Topeka, KS 66612
(913) 296-4945

Kentucky Bureau of Education for
Exceptional Children
Unit of Physically Handicapped
Capital Plaza Towers, Room 820
Frankfort, KY 40601
(502) 564-4970

Louisiana State Department of Education
Louisiana Learning Resources System
2525 Wyandotte Street
Baton Rouge, LA 70805
(504) 359-9285

Maine Department of Educational
and Cultural Services
State House Station #23
Augusta, ME 04333
(207) 289-5811

Maryland State Department of Education
200 West Baltimore Street
Baltimore, MD 21201
(301) 333-2489

Massachusetts Department of Education
Division of Special Education
Beaman Street, Route 140
West Boylston, MA 01583
(617) 835-6266

Michigan Department of Education
Special Education Services
P.O. Box 30008
Lansing, MI 48909
(517) 373-9433

Minnesota Department of Education
Unique Learning Center
812 Capitol Square Building
550 Cedar Street
St. Paul, MN 55101
(612) 296-4163

Mississippi Department of Education
Sillers State Office Building
Jackson, MS 39205
(601) 359-3513

Missouri Department of Elementary
and Secondary Education
P.O. Box 480
Jefferson City, MO 65102
(314) 751-4909

Montana Department of Educational Services
State Capitol, Room 106
Helena, MT 59620
(406) 444-4429

Nebraska Department of Education
301 Centennial Mall South
P.O. Box 94987
Lincoln, NE 68509
(402) 471-2471

Nevada Department of Education
400 West King Street
Carson City, NV 89710
(702) 885-3140

New Hampshire Department of Education
State Office Park South
101 Pleasant Street
Concord, NH 03301
(603) 271-3741

New Jersey Division of Special Education
225 West State Street
Trenton, NJ 08625
(609) 292-0147

New Mexico State Department of Education
Special Education Unit
300 Don Gaspar Street
Santa Fe, NM 87501-2786
(505) 827-6541

New York State Education Department
Office for Education of Children
with Handicapping Conditions
Education Building Annex, Room 1073
Albany, NY 12234
(518) 474-5548 or 474-8917

North Carolina Department of Public Instruction/
Division for Exceptional Children
Education Building
116 West Edenton Street
Raleigh, NC 27603-1712
(919) 733-3921

North Dakota Department of Public Instruction
State Capitol
Bismarck, ND 58505
(701) 224-2277

Ohio Department of Education
Division of Special Education
933 High Street
Worthington, OH 43085-4087
(614) 466-2650

Oklahoma State Department of Education
Special Education Section
Oliver Hodge Memorial Education Building
2500 North Lincoln
Oklahoma City, OK 73105
(405) 521-3351

Oregon Department of Education
700 Pringle Parkway, S.E.

Salem, OR 97301
(503) 378-2677

Pennsylvania Department of Education
Bureau of Special Education
Box 911, 333 Market Street
Harrisburg, PA 17108
(717) 783-6913

Puerto Rico Department of Education
Special Education Program
Box 759
Hato Rey, PR 00919
(809) 759-7228

Rhode Island Department of Education
22 Hayes Street
Providence, RI 02908
(401) 277-2031

South Carolina Department of Education
311 Rutledge Building
1429 Senate Street
Columbia, SC 29201
(803) 758-7432

South Dakota Division of Education
Section for Special Education
700 Governors Drive
Pierre, SD 57501-2293
(605) 773-3315

Tennessee Department of Education
132 Cordell Hull Building
Nashville, TN 37219
(615) 741-2851

Texas Education Agency
William B. Travis Building, Room 5-120
1701 North Congress Avenue
Austin, TX 78701
(512) 463-9414

Utah State Office of Education
Special Education Section
250 East Fifth South
Salt Lake City, UT 84111
(801) 533-5982

Vermont Division of Special and
Compensatory Education
Special Education Unit
State Office Building
120 State Street
Montpelier, VT 05602
(802) 828-3141

Virginia Department for the Visually Handicapped
Programs for Infants, Children, and Youth
397 Azalea Avenue
Richmond, VA 23227
(804) 371-3140

Virgin Islands Department of Education
State Director of Special Education
P.O. Box 6640
Charlotte Amalie
St. Thomas, VI 00801
(809) 773-1095

Washington Office of Superintendent of Public
Instruction
Division of Special Education Services
Old Capitol Building
Olympia, WA 98504
(206) 753-6733

West Virginia Department of Education
State Capitol Building
Building #6, Room B-304
1900 Washington Street East
Charleston, WV 25305
(304) 348-2696

Wisconsin Bureau for Exceptional Children
Division for Handicapped Children
and Pupil Services
P.O. Box 7841
125 South Webster Street
Madison, WI 53703
(608) 266-3522

Wyoming Department of Education
Hathaway Building, Second Floor
2300 Capitol Avenue
Cheyenne, WY 82002
(307) 777-7414

Assessing vision/low vision

The list of visual impairments presented in this appendix is not meant to be complete or all-inclusive.[1] Rather, it is offered as an example of the range of impairments that may be encountered. Many of the conditions listed may be congenital or adventitious. Full explanations and definitions of these and other conditions can be provided by a student's eye specialist.

The educational implications of an eye condition are an important factor in determining a student's needs. Interaction among the teacher of visually impaired students, the eye specialist, and the student's physician is essential in assessing and meeting the visually impaired student's unique educational needs in this area. The following visual impairments are among those that may be affecting a student's vision:

1. Irregularities of the optical media (e.g., cornea, lens, and aqueous and vitreous humors), such as keratoconus, irregular astigmatism, and lentiglobus, cause a distortion of the visual image, photophobia, or both and may cause monocular diplopia.
2. Medial opacities, such as cataracts, corneal scarring, and vitreous turbidity, may cause light deprivation, glare or scattering, loss of contrast, impaired color perception, diminished central visual acuity, monocular diplopia, or any combination of these conditions.
3. Extraocular motility defects resulting from strabismus or paresis may affect binocularity.
4. Defects of the iris and pupil include aniridia, polycoria (developmental, traumatic, or atrogenic), fixed pupil, and lack of pigmentation (as in albinism). These conditions may cause photophobia, monocular diplopia, or degradation of central vision.
5. Defects of cone (central) vision may cause inaccurate or total loss of color perception and diminished central visual acuity.
6. Defects of rod (peripheral) vision may cause reduced or total inability to adapt to low levels of illumination, complete or partial loss in peripheral vision, or both these conditions.
7. Defects of the optic nerve pathways or occipital cortex may cause a loss of central vision, color vision defects, or loss in peripheral vision, including scotomata, quadrantanopsia, or hemianopsia. These defects may affect one or both eyes, depending on the site of the defect, and may or may not be symmetrical between the two eyes.
8. Other types of vision loss due to intraocular origin include retinoschisis, retinal detachment, choroiditis, and glaucoma. These types of pathology cause a loss in visual field or diminished central or peripheral vision.
9. Systemic diseases have numerous ocular manifestations that are as varied as the disease entities themselves. Examples of systemic disease with ocular manifestations are diabetes, multiple sclerosis, vascular disease, and hydrocephalus.

FUNCTIONAL VISION ASSESSMENT
Visually impaired students need to learn to use their vision as efficiently as possible. To meet this need, the teacher of visually impaired students, in conjunction with the orientation and mobility specialist, should evaluate how the student uses his or her vision to function within the school setting and in the community. Parents can also provide valuable information about their child's use of vision.

Given these assessment data and the information from a form such as the "Eye Report for Children with Visual Problems" (a sample of which appears in this appendix), the individuals assessing a student typically prepare a functional vision checklist summary sheet, such as the one that appears in this appendix. This report contains recommendations for further assessment by an eye specialist, if needed.

On the basis of this assessment information, the teacher of visually impaired students and the orientation and mobility specialist will teach the student to adapt to the environment to maximize the functional use of vision. This adaptation will take the following factors into account:
• Control of lighting and glare factors

---

[1]Definitions of many of the terms used to describe these visual impairments appear in the glossary. For additional definitions, see R.T. Jose, ed., *Understanding Low Vision* (New York: American Foundation for the Blind, 1983); H.A. Stein, B.J. Slatt, and R.M. Stein, *Ophthalmic Terminology: Speller and Vocabulary Builder* (2d ed.; St. Louis, MO: C.V. Mosby Company, 1987); and D. Vaughn and T. Asbury, *General Ophthalmology* (11th ed.; Los Altos, CA: Lange Medical Publications, 1986).

- Preferred field of view and best gaze posture (eccentric viewing)
- Adaptations of reading materials, such as print size, contrast, use of color, fatigue factors, time adjustments, and the use of auditory or braille media
- Training in the use of prescribed low vision devices, including telescopes for travel
- Recommendations for nonprescription devices, such as specialized paper, pens, reading stands, and adapted materials and appliances for specialized classes.

The goal of the assessment is to enable the student to function as independently as possible within the school and the community.

Additional areas to be included in a functional vision assessment are considerations relating to orientation and mobility. Examples of these considerations include the following:

1. Recognition of illumination: overhead, at body level, from windows, and artifical lighting
2. Gross object recognition: shape, size, size of room, doorways, desks, chairs, tables, and objects that are at body level, overhanging, low, in front of, and to the side
3. Fine object and characteristic recognition: people; names and numbers on doors; objects such as books, typewriters, telephones, and coffee cups; wall displays; chalkboard color; and writing on chalkboard
4. Contrast recognition: floor or wall, door or wall, door closed or opened, carpet or flooring, window or wall, bulletin board or wall, and chalkboard or wall (objects: dark on light, light on dark, light on light, and dark on dark)
5. Print recognition: print on chalkboard—white chalk, colored chalk, blackboard, greenboard, beigeboard; print on paper—dark print and light paper, light print and dark paper, colored paper and dark print, and maps, charts, and graphs
6. Color recognition: floor, wall, blackboard, greenboard, beigeboard, objects, clothing, maps, charts, and graphs
7. Depth perception: ascending stairs, descending stairs, drop-offs, step-ups, inclines and declines, floor strips, and thresholds
8. Student in motion: line of travel; confidence; ability to locate doors and windows; recognition of intersecting hallways; travel through open doors; recognition of stairs, depth change, color, and changes in contrast; avoidance of people, overhangs, low objects, and objects at side.[2]

---

[2]*Note:* Additional evaluation of a student's use of vision outdoors should be carried out by the orientation and mobility specialist.

ASSESSMENT BY A QUALIFIED EYE SPECIALIST

An assessment by a fully qualified eye specialist should be performed to provide an understanding of the nature and extent of the student's vision loss. The following discussion summarizes the items needed in the eye specialist's report.

Detailed case history

A detailed case history should include the following:

- Exploration of the etiology of vision loss; age at onset
- "Historical landmarks" in the disease process
- Eye preference
- Patient's present visual abilities and deficits
- Patient's desires concerning visual rehabilitation
- Patient's concept of his or her goals (vocational, avocational, recreational, educational, daily living, and so forth)
- Past and present medical history
- Significant family medical history
- Patient's evaluation of environmental effects on vision (e.g., lighting)
- Stability of patient's vision (including any recent changes)
- History of patient's use of visual or nonvisual devices
- Patient's motivation
- Patient's attitude.

Visual acuity measurements

Distance visual acuity. Measurement of the student's distance vision should be done with and without present correction at a distance of 10 feet. This distance may need to be shortened in cases of severe vision loss. If distance low vision devices are used, an assessment of visual acuity and efficency in the use of the devices should be performed. An assessment of illumination effects should also be done.

Near visual acuity. The student's near visual acuity should be measured with and without present correction at the reading distance the student chooses. Acuities should be recorded, as well as the working distance. Any low vision devices the student presently has, as well as the effects of illumination, should be evaluated. If low vision devices are used in school or work, a measure of acuity and efficiency achieved should be done at the required working distance.

External examination

An evaluation of the ability of the eyes to track together and maintain fixation should be performed. The areas involved in an external examination are as follows:

Evaluation of extraocular motility. If strabismus is present, magnitude and comitancy should be measured. The student's head tilt or rotation should be checked. If nystagmus is present, it should be determined whether a change in amplitude occurs with a change in the direction of the student's gaze or whether a latent component exists.

Pupillary reflexes. An examination of pupillary reflexes can be employed to rule out neurological problems or to detect strabismus, for example, by using the Hirschberg Test. An estimation of the pupil's symmetry, size, shape, and position relative to the center of the cornea can be made. Transillumination of the iris should be performed to detect the degree of iris pigmentation present.

Color and stereopsis testing. The testing of color perception is the measurement of the eye's ability to discriminate various hues of color. Color perception can be tested using color plates and/or a Farnsworth-type test. Stereopsis can be evaluated as well, using a polaroid test (e.g., WIRT). If no stereopsis is present, gross fusion can be tested by anaglyph methods (e.g., the Worth Test). The student should be allowed to hold the test at his or her best near-working distance.

Keratometry. Keratometry is a measurement of curvature on the anterior surface of the cornea.

Retinoscopy. Retinoscopy is a method of objectively measuring refractive error by shining a light through the pupil and neutralizing its reflex with lenses. This procedure may need to be done at unusual working distances if hazy media or irregular refractive surfaces are present (radical retinoscopy).

Subjective testing

Subjective testing is a method of measuring refractive error by evaluating a student's response to changes in lens power. A trial frame and trial lenses should be used, rather than the refractor, to allow for eye or head movements. Testing by the ''Just Noticeable Differences'' (JND) method and a hand-held crossed cylinder should be done at a comfortable viewing distance for the student. For students with strong prescriptions, an overrefraction may be performed with the use of Halberg clips or similar devices. Visual acuity should be measured at the conclusion of the refraction, and testing of the effect of illumination on distance vision should be performed.

With the best-distance refraction in place, testing with various powered spectacle-mounted telescopes and hand-held monoculars should be performed. Monocular stands can also be evaluated. A refinement of the trial frame refraction should also be performed with a telescope in place.

Near-vision testing is generally performed after distance-vision testing is concluded. A reasonable starting point would be to calculate the reciprocal of vision to determine the approximate amount of magnification required. Starting with this amount of magnification, various powered lenses can be evaluated to provide relative distance magnification. For students with a severe vision loss, microscopic lenses can also be evaluated. Hand and stand magnifiers, loupes, closed-circuit television, reading stands, illumination devices, and other devices may be analyzed. If specific working distances are required, telemicroscopes, surgical telescopes, or alternative systems may be needed. Acuity should be measured with single- and multiple-digit print, as well as with the student's desired reading material.

Testing with an artificial iris or pupil contact lenses for students with albinism or who suffer from glare should be performed. Specially designed filters should be evaluated, such as NOIR or CPF. Various density and colored tints should be evaluated for both indoor and outdoor use. Visors, typoscopes, and single or multiple pinholes should also be considered, as well as devices to provide an increase in illumination. Visual field defects can be ameliorated by the use of field expanders (hand-held or spectacle-mounted), Fresnel prisms, or hemianopic mirrors.

Students with high refractive errors or nystagmus should be evaluated with contact lenses to determine whether a better visual result can be obtained. Students with scarred or irregular corneal surfaces may benefit from contact lens fit or minification, or lenses may be used as a light-filtering apparatus. Contact lenses may be used to provide magnification to transmit selectively particular wavelengths of light.

Objective testing

The following examples are means of objective testing:
- Biomicroscopy and tonometry
- Ophthalmoscopy
- Visual field assessment. Central defects may be charted on an Ansler Grid or tangent screen, with a large fixation cross present. Peripheral fields are best assessed on an arc perimeter or ''bowl type'' visual field testing instrument.

Considerations in prescribing low vision devices

The following factors should be considered by those prescribing low vision devices:

- Student's goals, desires, and needs
- Working distances required
- Illumination requirements
- Field of view needed
- Age of student
- Use of multiple devices
- Stability of vision
- Performance with various devices tested.

Supplementary low vision services and needs
The following supplementary low vision needs should also be considered:

- The training of the student in the use of low vision devices
- The monitoring of the student for a change in visual status.

The National Accreditation Council for Agencies Serving the Blind and Visually Handicapped (see Appendix A for address) has developed standards for low vision clinics that readers may wish to obtain. In addition, readers may find helpful the samples of eye reports and related forms provided in the remainder of this appendix.

EXAMPLE OF REGISTRATION FORM
USED BY STATE DEPARTMENT OF EDUCATION

Registration of visually handicapped students, as of January 2, 19____

Check one: ☐Public school   ☐Nonpublic school

_____

Name of the school district, office of the county superintendent of schools, or nonpublic school

_____

Street address   City   Zip code   County

_____   _____

Name of authorized officer   Title

_____   ( )_____

Address, if different from the central office   Telephone number

_____

Date

Total number of legally blind students reported: _____

Total number of partially sighted students reported: _____

I certify that information contained in this registration is based on current eye report forms retained by this office. To establish eligibility for the American Printing House for the Blind Federal Quota Program, I further certify that this school system has filed with the Department of Education an Assurance of Compliance Statement, based on the Civil Rights Act of 1964.

                                    _____

                                    Signature of authorized officer

Return this form to:

65

EXAMPLE OF EYE REPORT FORM OFTEN USED
BY STATE DEPARTMENTS OF EDUCATION

CONFIDENTIAL EYE REPORT FOR CHILDREN WITH VISUAL PROBLEMS R L B

NAME OF PUPIL_____ SEX _____ RACE _____
(Type or print)   (First)   (Middle)   (Last)

ADDRESS_____ DATE OF BIRTH _____
        (No. and street)   (City or town)   (County)   (State)   (Month) (Day) (Year)

GRADE_____ SCHOOL _____ ADDRESS _____

I. HISTORY

A. Probable age at onset of vision impairment. Right eye (O.D.)_____ Left eye (O.S.) _____

B. Severe ocular infections, injuries, operations, if any, with age at time of occurrence _____
_____

C. Has pupil's ocular condition occurred in any blood relative(s)? _____ If so, what relationship(s)? _____

II. MEASUREMENTS (See back of form for preferred notation for recording visual acuity and table of approximate equivalents.)

A. VISUAL ACUITY

	DISTANT VISION			NEAR VISION			PRESCRIPTION		
	Without correction	With best correction*	With low vision aid	Without correction	With best correction*	With low vision aid	Sph.	Cyl.	Axis
Right eye (O.D.)	_____	_____	_____	_____	_____	_____	_____	_____	_____
Left eye (O.S.)	_____	_____	_____	_____	_____	_____	_____	_____	_____
Both eyes (O.U.)	_____	_____	_____	_____	_____	_____	Date _____		

B. If glasses are to be worn, were safety lenses prescribed in: Plastic_____ Tempered glass_____   *with ordinary lenses

C. If low vision aid is prescribed, specify type and recommendations for use._____
_____

D. FIELD OF VISION: Is there a limitation? _____ If so, record results of test on chart on back of form.

What is the widest diameter (in degrees) of remaining visual field? O.D. _____ O.S. _____

E. Is there impaired color perception? _____ If so, for what color(s)?_____

III. CAUSE OF BLINDNESS OR VISION IMPAIRMENT

A. Present ocular condition(s) responsible for vision impairment. (If more than one, specify all but underline the one which probably first caused severe vision impairment.)

O.D._____

O.S._____

B. Preceding ocular condition, if any, which led to present condition, or the underlined condition, specified in A.

O.D._____

O.S._____

C. Etiology (underlying cause) of ocular condition primarily responsible for vision impairment. (e.g., specific disease, injury, poisoning, heredity or other prenatal influence.)

O.D._____

O.S._____

D. If etiology is injury or poisoning, indicate circumstances and kind of object or poison involved. _____
_____

IV. PROGNOSIS AND RECOMMENDATIONS

A. Is pupil's vision impairment considered to be: Stable_____ Deteriorating_____ Capable of improvement_____ Uncertain_____

B. What treatment is recommended, if any?_____

C. When is reexamination recommended? _____

D. Glasses: Not needed _____ To be worn constantly _____ For close work only_____ Other (specify)_____

E. Lighting requirements: Average_____ Better than average_____ Less than average_____

F. Use of eyes: Unlimited_____ Limited, as follows:_____

G. Physical activity: Unrestricted _____ Restricted, as follows: _____

TO BE FORWARDED BY EXAMINER TO:

Date of examination_____

Signature of examiner _____ Degree_____

Address_____

If clinic case: Number_____ Name of clinic _____

(Continued on next page)

PREFERRED VISUAL ACUITY NOTATIONS

DISTANT VISION. Use Snellen notation with test distance of 20 feet. (Examples: 20/100, 20/60). For acuities less than 20/200 record distance at which 200 foot letter can be recognized as numerator of fraction and 200 as denominator. (Examples: 10/200, 3/200). If the 200 foot letter is not recognized at 1 foot record abbreviation for best distant vision as follows:

HM	HAND MOVEMENTS
PLL	PERCEIVES AND LOCALIZES LIGHT IN ONE OR MORE QUADRANTS
LP	PERCEIVES BUT DOES NOT LOCALIZE LIGHT
No LP	NO LIGHT PERCEPTION

NEAR VISION. Use standard A.M.A. notation and specify best distance at which pupil can read. (Example: 14/70 at 5 in.)

TABLE OF APPROXIMATE EQUIVALENT VISUAL ACUITY NOTATIONS

These notations serve only as an indication of the approximate relationship between recordings of distant and near vision and point type sizes. The teacher will find in practice that the pupil's reading performance may vary considerably from the equivalents shown.

Distant Snellen	Near A.M.A.	Near Jaeger	Near Metric	% Central Visual Efficiency for Near	Point	Usual Type Text Size
20/20 (ft.)	14/14 (in.)	1	0.37 (M.)	100	3	Mail order catalogue
20/30	14/21	2	0.50	95	5	Want ads
20/40	14/28	4	0.75	90	6	Telephone directory
20/50	14/35	6	0.87	50	8	Newspaper text
20/60	14/42	8	1.00	40	9	Adult text books
20/80	14/56	10	1.50	20	12	Children's books 9-12 yrs
20/100	14/70	11	1.75	15	14	Children's books 8-9 yrs.
20/120	14/84	12	2.00	10	18 }	
20/200	14/140	17	3.50	2	24 }	Large type text
12.5/200	14/224	19	6.00	1.5		
8/200	14/336	20	8.00	1		
5/200	14/560					
3/200	14/900					

FIELD OF VISION. Record results on chart below.

Type of test used: _____   Illumination in ft. candles: _____

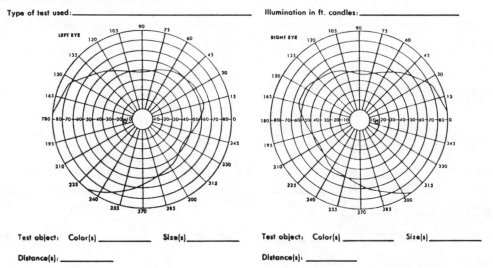

Test object: Color(s) _____ Size(s) _____   Test object: Color(s) _____ Size(s) _____

Distance(s): _____   Distance(s): _____

EXAMPLE OF FUNCTIONAL VISION CHECKLIST

Functional Vision Checklist Summary Sheet

Date_____

Student_____ Age _____ Grade _____ School _____

Vision Teacher_____ Contact Phone_____Room

PHYSICAL INFORMATION

Nature of eye condition (describe in simple terms)_____

_____

Educational implications of eye condition _____

_____

Glasses prescribed _____ To be worn _____

Describe prescription (bifocal, aphakic, contact lens)_____

_____

Acuity (Near vision) _____ Field _____

Acuity (Far vision)_____ Color vision _____

Preferred eye_____ Child is/is not binocular _____

Preferred field of view _____ Best gaze posture, if any _____

_____

Photophobia _____ Sunshade prescribed _____

CLASSROOM MODIFICATIONS: DISTANCE VISION

Child can use:

Overhead projectors_____ Flipcharts_____

Filmstrips _____ Flashcards _____

Television _____Wall clock _____

Blackboard: Child should be seated

In front row_____Right front_____ Left front _____Other _____

Distance aids used_____

Time adjustments (such as extra time to copy from blackboard)_____

_____

_____

(Continued on next page)

CLASSROOM MODIFICATIONS: NEAR TASKS

1. Reading

Optimum reading time _____

Child prefers to improve visual functioning by (finger pointing, marker, etc.) _____

Child's grade level when reading print _____

Print size   Reading_____   Mathematics_____

               Activity books _____   Ditto papers _____

               Dictionary _____   Other _____

Adaptations of reading materials _____

_____

2. Near vision devices

Use of optical devices _____

Reading stand_____   Marking pen_____   Writing paper_____

Ditto filters _____   Typoscope/marker _____

Closed-circuit television (CCTV):

Best magnification _____   Polarity _____   Reading distance _____

Special lighting required _____

Auditory (listening) program_____

Child's grade level for auditory reading _____

Type of classwork to be read by ear _____

_____

EQUIPMENT ADAPTATIONS FOR CLASSES

Will the student need special adaptations in:

Cooking_____   Sewing_____   Shop_____

Laboratory _____   Physical education _____

Testing situations: Modifications required (time and materials) _____

_____

TRAVEL SKILLS

Student is oriented to: School _____   Bus _____   Community _____

Can travel independently _____

Adaptations for independent travel _____

Time adjustments for travel _____

Additional notes: _____

Reprinted from Sally S. Mangold, ed., *A Teacher's Guide to the Special Educational Needs of Blind and Visually Handicapped Children* (New York: American Foundation for the Blind, 1982).

EXAMPLE OF EYE REPORT FORM

Educationally Oriented Vision Report

(To be completed by the eye specialist)

Date: Month   Day   Year   Student's name: Last   First   Middle

The following information would be helpful in determining educational programming based on the needs of the student. We would appreciate your completing this form in addition to the "Eye Report for Children with Visual Problems."

1. What is the cause of visual impairment?

2. Is any special treatment required? If so, what is the general nature of the treatment?

3. Is the visual impairment likely to get worse, better, or stay the same?

4. What symptoms would indicate a need for reexamination?

5. Should any restrictions be placed on the student's activities?

6. Should the student wear glasses or contact lenses? If so, under what circumstances?

7. If it was not possible to do a visual acuity measure, what is your opinion regarding what the student sees?

8. Are the student's focusing ability, tracking, and eye muscle balance adequate? If not, please describe:

9. If the student's visual field was not testable, what is your opinion regarding this student's field of vision?

10. Please describe the object size and distances that are optimal for the student:

11. What lighting conditions would be optimal for the student's visual functioning?

12. Do you have any additional specific recommendations concerning this student's use of vision in learning situations?

13. When should this student be examined again?

Please return this form to:

Reprinted from *Program Guidelines for Visually Impaired Individuals* (rev. ed.; Sacramento, CA: California State Department of Education, 1987).

Position papers, Council for Exceptional Children

As a result of the efforts of the Professional Standards Committee of the Council for Exceptional Children's Division for the Visually Handicapped, the council compiled a series of statements about essential elements in high-quality educational programming for visually impaired students. Six of these statements about key areas of concern are reprinted with the council's permission in this appendix.

THE ROLE AND FUNCTION OF THE TEACHER OF THE VISUALLY HANDICAPPED

Susan Jay Spungin
American Foundation for the Blind

Now more than ever before the field is seeing a need to define the role and function of teachers of the visually handicapped, especially in light of the growing acceptance of the generic special education program models and personnel developed to serve the low incidence population of visually handicapped children. In order to justify the need for trained teachers in vision to serve these children the field must be very clear as to what is actually meant by "a teacher of the visually handicapped." Consequently, what follows are areas of specialized activities to serve as role guidelines for teacher/consultants of the visually handicapped in community day school programs.

I. **Assessment and evaluation**
   A. Perform functional vision assessments.
   B. Obtain and interpret eye/medical reports as they relate to educational environments.
   C. Contribute to appropriate portions of the IEP, such as long-term goals, short-term goals, learning style/ physical constraints.
   D. Recommend appropriate service delivery plans, including physical education, ancillary support services, equipment, time frames.

Reprinted with permission from *Quality Services for Blind and Visually Handicapped Learners: Statements of Position* (Reston, VA: Division for the Visually Handicapped, Council for Exceptional Children, 1984).

   E. Recommend appropriate specialized evaluations as needed, such as low vision, orientation and mobility, psychological, and adaptive physical education.
   F. Confer with special services to aid in evaluation.
   G. Assist in determining the eligibility and the appropriate placement of visually handicapped children.
   H. Participate in the assessment of each pupil, and interpret results to classroom teachers and others.

II. **Educational and instructional strategies: learning environment**
   A. Assure that the student is trained in the use of, and has available, all devices and technological apparatus useful to the process of academic learning.
   B. Assure that the classroom teacher fully understands the unique needs of children with visual losses.
   C. Act as a catalyst in developing understanding of visual loss with sighted children.
   D. Interpret adjustments needed in assignments or standards in the regular classroom.
   E. Assure that the student has all educational materials in the appropriate media.
   F. Consult with the classroom teachers regarding methodology to be used as visually handicapped children are included in classroom learning experiences.
   G. Instruct the student in academic subjects and activities requiring adaptation and reinforcement as a direct result of visual handicap.

III. **Educational and instructional strategies: unique curriculum**
   A. Braille Reading and Writing—It may be necessary for the teacher of the visually handicapped to provide beginning braille reading instruction and to introduce the child to such mechanical aspects of reading as: top of the page, bottom of the page, use of fingers, tracking, etc. Introduction of writing is also the responsi-

bility of the teacher of the visually handicapped. Braille writers and slates and styli are unfamiliar learning tools to the classroom teacher; the classroom teacher should not be expected to master the mechanics of either. The teacher of the visually handicapped will possess the necessary skills in braille mathematics and in braille music, and will provide instruction to students in their use.

B. Handwriting—For the partially seeing child, certain aspects of handwriting in respect to size and configuration may be the responsibility of the teacher of the visually handicapped. The teaching of signature writing, and, if appropriate, additional handwriting skills to functionally blind children is certainly a responsibility.

C. Typewriting—For most low vision children and functionally blind children typing will be the major means of communication between the child and sighted peers, parents, and teachers. This is a skill which should be carefully and thoroughly taught by the teacher of the visually handicapped as soon as the pupil has sufficient motor skills.

D. Large Print and Optical Aids—It may be necessary for the teacher of the visually handicapped to help low vision children utilize reading aids in order to fully benefit in the regular classroom.

E. Listening Skills—Both partially seeing and functionally blind students need to learn good listening skills. Listening becomes extremely important in the secondary grades when print reading assignments become long and laborious. It is necessary for the visually handicapped child to begin a sequential course of study in the development of listening skills as early as possible. The development of listening skills is not confined to the use of an alternate reading system. It is important in mobility, in social conversation, and in interpreting a variety of auditory signals received from the environment.

F. Study Skills—Skimming braille or large print materials, outlining in braille or large print, searching for significant information in recorded materials, and other skills may need to be taught by the teacher of the visually handicapped.

G. Tactual Skills—The development of tactual skills is not confined to the reading of braille. Visually handicapped students should be taught to use their fingers and hands well in order to explore, identify, and appreciate all tangible materials in their environment.

H. Visual Efficiency—This underlines achievement in every skill area for the partially seeing pupil: academic, psychomotor skills, self-help, and vocational and social skills. The use of residual vision is one of the most important aspects of the curriculum offered by the teacher of the visually handicapped.

I. Motor Development—The teacher of the visually handicapped must know the potential problem areas in motor development for visually handicapped children. Body image, body in space concepts, visual motor skills, etc., are included in this area.

J. Physical Education—This is often a problem for visually handicapped pupils in public schools. Students must be assisted in understanding and participating in team games. Physical fitness must be stressed.

K. Orientation and Mobility—Much of the orientation and mobility needs of the student are the responsibility of qualified orientation and mobility instructors. The responsibilities of, and the relationship between the teachers of the visually handicapped and orientation and mobility instructors must be clearly defined. It is possible that the former will assume responsibility for assuring that students develop in sensory motor, gross, and fine motor skills. Visually handicapped children must be taught to move in space and to be aware of the environment around them. They must learn to use tactual and auditory cues to assist and identify their position in space and the relative position of other persons and objects around them.

L. Concept Development—The teacher of the visually handicapped shares with others the responsibility for the development of basic concepts by the student. Future learning is dependent upon the student's thorough understanding and association, discrimination, and relationships.

M. Activities of Daily Living—Thorough knowledge of the activities and techniques of daily living or personal management skills is needed to create independence so that visually handicapped students may become acceptable and personable beings—free of mannerisms, and socially attractive to others. Specific objectives include but are not limited to: a) caring for personal needs; b) developing adequate eating habits; c) mastering the process and routine of dressing and undressing; d) developing a positive self-image.

N. Reasoning—The ability to reason, especially in the abstract, may require specific instruction from the teacher of the visually handicapped. Students may need assistance in the development of decision-making skills, problem solving, and learning to live with occasional frustration and failure.

O. Human Sexuality—Teachers of the visually handicapped, parents and others share the responsibility for gradual, sequential instruction in human sexuality for visually handicapped students. Because programs in sex education for sighted children assume that much visual information has been previously attained, the visually handicapped pupil may need a specific curriculum taught by appropriate, well-prepared professionals.

P. Leisure and Recreation—The teacher of the visually handicapped, parents, and community agencies share a responsibility to expose the student to, and provide learning opportunities in, a wide variety of leisure time activities which have carry-over value to adult life.

IV. Guidance and counseling

A. Guidance and counseling assists visually handicapped students in understanding their attitudes and those of others concerning visual impairment; in exploring similarities and differences in relation to all children; in becoming socially aware of oneself and environment; in learning acceptable behavior; in encouraging social interactions with peer groups; and in becoming more independent. Parents should be included in this guidance and counseling process.

B. Career education curriculum that has been developed for sighted children may need supplementary instruction from a teacher of the visually handicapped. Career education encompasses three sequential areas: career awareness, career exploration, and vocational preparation. Each, in sequence, is dependent upon the other. A curriculum in career education for the visually handicapped may be necessary, and implementation of this curriculum may be the responsibility of the teacher of the visually handicapped. At the career exploration level this could well mean many field trips into the community so that the visually handicapped student will have exposure to people and work situations.

C. Vocational counseling is an integral part of programs designed for visually handicapped students. Career awareness begins on the primary level, continuing with career exploration and orientation on the intermediate and secondary level. The teacher in conjunction with the counselor should involve visually handicapped students and parents in this counseling process. Following the assessment of vocational strengths and weaknesses, the students may participate in work-study experience programs as appropriate.

D. Social adjustment skills are an integral part of the curriculum and assist the visually handicapped student to blend smoothly into society. Areas that must be emphasized are spatial awareness and orientation, verbal and nonverbal language, self-help skills, socialization processes, interpersonal relations, human sexuality, and real life experiences.

E. Support services to families should include:
   1. Interpreting implications of visual impairment on overall development;
   2. Referring to appropriate service providers;
   3. Encouraging home involvement in program objectives;
   4. Acting as a resource in the field of vision.

V. Administration and supervision

A. Communication with Administrators
   1. Pupil information (e.g., visual status, grade level, prototype).
   2. Program goals and activities.
   3. Program evaluation.
   4. Screening and referral procedures.
   5. Relationship to other regular and special education programs and support services.
   6. Budget funds to include funds for travel time, consultation, instruction, salaries, travel expenses, instructional materials, preparation time, conferences and benefits.

7. In-service programs by and for teacher/consultants of the visually impaired.
8. Program scheduling to allow adequate time for planning, preparation, reporting, commuting, instruction and staff conferences.
9. Physical facilities which include instructional settings, offices and storage space.
10. Advocate of students' educational/legal rights and provider of services.
11. Provide input into scheduling of students.

B. Record Keeping
1. Maintain statewide and system-wide student census.
2. Obtain and maintain student medical and optometric reports.
3. Maintain records of pupil assessments, individual educational plans, reviews and progress reports with signed parental release forms.
4. Maintain material and equipment requests.

C. Casefinding, Student Referral Procedures and Scheduling
1. Act as a vision consultant for system-wide screening, materials, follow-up and recommendations.
2. Participate in LEA's annual plan for Child Search.
3. Maintain a referral/communication system with nurses and other school staff.
4. Obtain current eye reports and begin notification and assessment.
5. Schedule time for teaching, planning, preparation, travel, and conferences with parents and relevant school and non-school persons.
6. Maintain records and exchange information about visually handicapped students with appropriate personnel and consistent with school district policies regarding confidentiality.
7. Prepare a master schedule to be given to the supervisor and the principal of the building in which students are served.
8. Work within the framework and policies of the school.

VI. School community relations
A. School and Community Involvement—The teacher of the visually handicapped should be prepared to interpret the program to school personnel, board of education, and other groups within the community.
B. Program Liaison
1. Private, state and local agencies and schools.
2. Resources within the community.
3. Medical specialists.
4. Placement transitions.
5. Parents.
6. Related appropriate specialists.
7. Recreation resources.
C. Services Development
1. Coordinate ancillary groups and individuals, such as transcribers, recordists, readers for visually handicapped students, counselors and mobility instructors.
2. Assist in the initiation of new services as well as coordinating existing ones to bring the varied and necessary related services to the educational program.
3. Attend professional meetings (in and out of the district) concerned with the education of visually handicapped students.
4. Keep abreast of new developments in the education of visually handicapped children and youth.
5. Maintain on-going contact with parents to assure realistic understanding of child's abilities, progress, future goals, community resources, etc.

THE ROLE AND RESPONSIBILITY OF THE STATE EDUCATION CONSULTANT FOR THE VISUALLY HANDICAPPED

Adopted by the State Education Consultants for the Visually Handicapped

In order that visually handicapped children and youth may be assured of receiving a free, appropriate, public education of consistently high quality, state departments of education must maintain at least one full-time consultant specifically trained and experienced in education of the visually handicapped and assigned responsibility for educational programming for visually handicapped children and youth.

Since the 1940s there have been persons in state departments of education with titles similar to "state education consultant for the visually handicapped." From the beginning, these persons were primary advocates to insure appropriate acceptance of the visually handicapped child into the regular education program. Later in the 1960s, they expanded their activities to include conducting inservice training programs and setting up specialized materials centers. Throughout the three decades, state consultants were instrumental in the development and coordination of volunteer services to produce textbooks and other specialized educational materials. During the 1970s, state special education laws and federal legislation, particularly Public Law 94-142, The Education of All Handicapped Children Act, brought new challenges, increased demands, and major changes in the role and responsibilities of the state education consultants for the visually handicapped.

Presently, the necessity for continuation of a strong coordination and support role within state departments of education specifically for programs and services to visually handicapped children and youth is a low priority for many state education leaders. The need for these state consultants' specialized skills is frequently unrecognized in spite of their long and successful history of encouraging the integration of visually handicapped students into regular education programs. In addition, services for the visually handicapped must often compete with higher incidence handicapped populations and previously unserved populations for representation and funds.

Public Law 94-142 and Section 504 of Public Law 94-112 have had a tremendous impact on the role and responsibilities of leadership personnel in all special education categorical areas. In most states, the implementation of these laws has demanded changes in function for state department personnel. They are shifting from responsibility for particular program areas such as vision to monitoring compliance with state and federal regulations. However, if the quality of programs for visually handicapped students at the local level is not to be eroded, concerned professionals must define roles and responsibilities that are essential to the effective functioning of state education consultants for the visually handicapped so that creative leadership may be provided to the local school districts. To assure the free, appropriate, public education for all visually handicapped students, state education consultants for the visually handicapped children and youth are necessary to:

- Serve as advocates for the formation and implementation of appropriate laws, regulations, and program standards affecting the educational well-being of all visually handicapped students;
- Provide leadership to teachers in local and regional education programs and to function as advocates for them with local administrators;
- Provide an on-going program of local administrative professional development in order to raise the level of technical expertise for those local supervisors responsible for making important daily programmatic decisions;
- Serve as catalysts for the development of teacher-designed inservice opportunities;
- Serve as consultants to local school district personnel as they conduct appropriately designed program evaluation and improvement practices;
- Design and administer sytematic child search plans which will effectively identify students needing specialized educational services related to visual handicaps;
- Act as analysts of census data in order to recommend and enforce the establishment of a continuum of appropriate program models to serve all identified students, regardless of the students' educational level or geographic location;
- Assure that adequate federal, state, and local funding programs are provided to support state-wide special education delivery systems;
- Serve as advocates for the development and maintenance of comprehensive delivery systems for specialized educational materials and equipment to support visually handicapped students in the least restrictive settings;
- Assure that appropriate related services are provided as necessary within the special education delivery systems;
- Design and administer public communication systems which will clearly describe all programs and services potentially necessary for visually handicapped students to receive a free, appropriate, public education;
- Serve to foster interagency, intra-agency, and medical community cooperation to insure the smooth provision of other necessary social, vocational, rehabilitation, medical, and welfare services to visually handicapped students in concert with the total educational system;
- Serve as information channels to the U.S. Education Department, Office of Special Education and Rehabilitation Services in the long range development of appropriate programs, services, and technology;
- Advise teacher-training institutions of evolving competencies needed for teachers of the visually handicapped; and
- Maintain regular communication with national professional organizations and consumer groups to insure

uniformity of service delivery patterns and to keep abreast of the latest policy, curricular, technological and program developments.

To perform these tasks, and to function adequately as leaders, state education consultants for the visually handicapped must have a background of knowledge and understanding about the special educational needs of visually handicapped students and must possess skill in administration and consultation. The following competencies are considered to be essential:

- Ability to design and implement an appropriate special education service delivery system for all visually handicapped students;
- Ability to supervise, advocate for, coordinate, and support teachers who work with visually handicapped students at the local and regional levels;
- Skill to assess, determine priorities, and manage time and resources;
- Ability to secure funds and manage fiscal matters;
- Ability to utilize skills of a change agent to establish appropriate service delivery systems;
- Ability to plan and implement on-going staff development;
- Ability to work effectively with other professionals such as local and state education officials, instructional materials center personnel, legislators, college/university personnel, parents, community volunteers, etc.;
- Ability to engage in meaningful problem solving;
- Skill in analyzing and utilizing the political communications systems;
- Ability to serve in an advocacy role;
- Ability to apply research skills to the solution of educational problems;
- Ability to select and manage appropriate evaluation procedures for handicapped students and programs; and
- Skill in facilitation and consultation.

With these competencies, a state education consultant can serve in an advocacy role to assure that visually handicapped children and youth are adequately represented at state and national levels. To do so effectively, however, requires that the primary foci and priorities of the state education consultant for visually handicapped be to assure that appropriate special education delivery systems for the visually handicapped exist and to provide support critically necessary for teachers and administrators at the local and regional levels.

INSTRUCTIONAL RESOURCE CENTERS FOR THE VISUALLY HANDICAPPED

Julie Holton Todd, Ohio Resource Center for Low Incidence and Severely Handicapped

Specialized materials and equipment are a necessary and vital component of the education of children with visual impairments. Time, effective and efficient use of monies, and knowledge of resources are essential considerations when designing a system of delivering materials and services to visually handicapped students.

Textbooks in braille, large print, and/or on tape are costly items that are most often needed by a student for only 1 year before a new grade-level text is needed. Locating titles in the appropriate format is a time-consuming process that requires knowledge of local, state, and national resources. In addition, visually handicapped students often need specialized equipment such as braillewriters and tactual aids for mathematics, science, and other curricular areas. These items are not "on the shelves" of most school districts, and therefore they are not readily available when needed by students.

The most cost-effective way to deliver materials to students is through a statewide instructional resource center for the visually handicapped (IRC/VH). Such a delivery system can assist the state and local education agencies in the delivery of materials and services to visually handicapped students, their parents, and educators. IRC/VH's allow savings in staff time and money since items are easily located using established networks. Monies are used more effectively because items are recirculated and duplicate items are not purchased.

There are many types of delivery systems or IRC/VH models. Most states that have an IRC/VH system base the delivery system on one or more of the models listed below.

Acquisition/delivery model
- Receive requests for titles.
- Arrange for purchase and shipment of materials to the requester.

Clearinghouse model
- Receive requests for titles.
- Arrange for purchase and shipment of materials to the requester.
- Maintain an inventory system.
- Recirculate materials.

Depository model

- Receive requests for titles.
- Arrange for purchase and shipment of materials to the requester.
- Maintain an inventory system.
- Reuse materials.
- House materials in a central and/or satellite location.
- Return materials to the central or satellite location until they are needed again.

In addition to the services listed above, an IRC/VH may also offer the following:
- Information dissemination.
- Materials production in appropriate media for visually handicapped learners.
- Materials duplication in alternate media.
- Inservice and professional development for a variety of professionals and parents.
- Publication and dissemination of newsletters for professionals and parents.

Instructional resource centers for the visually handicapped are an effective way to use limited local, state, and federal monies to deliver appropriate materials and services to visually handicapped students in a timely manner. They provide the necessary textbooks in the required media as well as other specialized equipment and educational aids that may be necessary for these children to be able to properly function in their classrooms and to succeed as independent individuals in the sighted world.

THE ROLE OF RESIDENTIAL SCHOOLS FOR THE BLIND IN EDUCATING VISUALLY HANDICAPPED PUPILS

William H. Miller, Texas School for the Blind

Residential schools have historically possessed a proud leadership role in the education of blind and visually handicapped students. To continue this vital function, residential schools for the blind should continue to assume an innovative and dynamic leadership role in the development and delivery of appropriate quality educational programs for visually handicapped school-age children in concert with the state education agency, teacher training institutions, local school districts, parents, consumers, and other state and private organizations. The residential school can serve both the visually handicapped child and the child's parents as a direct service provider and as a most knowledgeable advocate

of the delivery of high quality educational services.

Because of the range and wealth of expertise located within the residential school, it should also function as the primary catalyst within the state to promote excellence in and relevance of the educational services provided in the public school sector through vigorous outreach efforts. The residential school should be viewed as a principal resource to local school programs by providing technical assistance, diagnostic and evaluation services, consultation, and direct services to children and families.

Directly related to its role as a provider of educationally appropriate programs, the residential school, because of its relatively large population of visually handicapped students, should also serve as a research and demonstration facility through which new and improved methods of delivering educational services to these learners can be developed. Innovative methods must be developed to apply the most advanced medical, educational, instructional, scientific, technological, psychological, and social knowledge to address the needs of blind and visually handicapped children.

Residential schools should provide supportive programs designed to meet the needs of students enrolled in public school programs. Intensive instruction should be offered in areas that may be minimally available at the local level such as orientation and mobility, independent living skills, use of technological devices, adaptive physical education, unique reading and math skills, vocational training, and productive use of leisure time. Also important is the oppportunity to socialize with peers who have similar disabilities.

Residential schools have recently begun to serve and should continue serving children who possess handicaps in addition to the visual impairment. Some of the finest programs for deaf-blind students are located at residential schools. The provision of services to multiply handicapped, visually handicapped students at residential schools is a vital role and should continue to be expanded as necessary.

Residential schools should advocate the placement of student interns at their institutions and be actively involved in the teacher training programs offered in their states and throughout the United States. Prospective teachers of visually handicapped students should be required to intern in residential and public school settings for exposure to both learning environments.

The educational programs at residential schools for the blind are characterized by knowledge of the unique needs and characteristics of visually handicapped students; awareness of the impacts of the home, school, and community on the development of the individual student; instruction in nonacademic areas such as dressing, eating, grooming, and orientation and mobility, opportunities to actively participate in extracurricular sports and recreational activities, and the ample availability of adaptive equipment and accessible facilities. It is important that the residential school is an educational setting that maintains a professional staff with specialized training and skills in the field of education of visually handicapped students.

The residential school for the blind should be viewed as one of a variety of components in an array of service delivery models, rather than as one of several options along a continuum of possible educational placements. While it is indeed true that a child may be away from his or her family for a week or more, the scope, intensity, and quality of the instructional services tailored exclusively for visually handicapped students delivered at such schools may very well define residential schools as an appropriate placement in the educational array of services. The residential school is a viable option for visually handicapped students for both short- and long-range services throughout their school careers. In most states there exists an extensive array of services for visually handicapped school-age children and their parents.

Components of the array of services include resource and itinerant programs offered through local school districts or special education cooperatives; support and consultative services from regional education service centers; administrative, regulatory, consultative, and fiscal support from the state education agency; and direct instructional, support, assessment, residential care, and consultative services delivered by the residential school. These service providers should coexist statewide in mutual support of the effort to insure to the maximum extent possible that comprehensive services are available to meet the unique educational needs of visually impaired students.

The residential school is usually the agency charged with the responsibility to provide comprehensive educational services on a residential basis to blind and visually handicapped students as well as perform the statewide functions indicated in the preceding paragraphs. Therefore, it should continue to serve as a very accessible resource to visually handicapped, multiply handicapped children and youth, their parents, local education agencies, and other state agencies, and to act as an agent to promote and, most importantly, to provide educational programs and services designed to meet these students' unique needs and learning characteristics.

EXPANSION OF THE ROLE OF THE TEACHER OF THE VISUALLY HANDICAPPED: PROVIDING FOR MULTI-IMPAIRED STUDENTS

Phil Vedovatti, Coordinator, Visually Impaired, Northwestern Illinois Association
Rosanne K. Silberman, Associate Professor, Hunter College of the City University of N.Y.

All multi-impaired students who have visual handicaps are entitled to the services of a trained teacher of the visually handicapped. Due to the increasing numbers of these students enrolling in day and residential school programs, educators of the visually handicapped should expand their roles, functions, and competencies. Many teachers are currently expected to serve children who have visual impairments in addition to a broad range of other disabilities including cerebral palsy, hearing impairment, mental retardation, and various neurological syndromes. Meeting the complex educational needs of these multi-impaired, visually handicapped (MI-VH) children in a wide variety of settings offers a unique challenge, which is the focus of this position paper.

It is the position of the DVH membership that all teachers of the visually handicapped have the competencies outlined in the publication: *Vision Field Must Define Teacher's Role, Function* (Spungin, 1979). These competencies include the areas of:

A. Assessment and Evaluation
B. Educational and Instructional Strategies
C. Learning Environment
D. Unique Curriculum
E. Guidance and Counseling
F. Administration and Supervision
G. School and Community Relations

Moreover, additional specific competencies now should be added to take into account the needs of MI-VH learners.

In the two areas, Assessment and Evaluation and Educational and Instructional Strategies, it is the primary responsibility of the professionals in the field of the education of the visually handicapped, especially teachers, to assess and develop, insofar as possible, functional vision skills in all multi-impaired students regardless of the severity or multiplicity of impairments. Of critical importance is having competencies in the following areas:

A. Knowledge of the common types of visual functioning difficulties in various handicapped populations
B. Knowledge of the effects of visual loss on language development
C. Knowledge of abnormal reflex and movement patterns and their interaction with visual functioning
D. Knowledge of appropriate positioning and handling techniques for multi-impaired students
E. Knowledge of the effects of visual loss on the performance of functional vision tasks, i.e., feeding activities, workshop tasks, manual communication skills, and the proper scanning of communication boards

While certain subject areas in which teachers of the visually handicapped should be trained are enumerated in the DVH position paper developed by Spungin (1979), the emphasis of these competencies is dramatically different when the focus is on education of the MI-VH student. These differences are particularly evident in the following areas:

A. Educational Assessment and Diagnosis
B. Leisure and Recreation
C. Human Sexuality
D. Motor Development
E. Cognitive Development
F. Social Adjustment Skills
G. Career and Vocational Education

Other areas of knowledge needed by teachers who work with multi-impaired students include:

A. Early child development with specific emphasis on normal and abnormal motor and language development
B. Augmentative communication systems
C. Principles of behavior management
D. Legislation and litigation related to children's rights to an education
E. Task analysis relevant to low functioning students

Visually handicapped students with multi-impairments are participating more frequently in diverse educational service delivery models and living successfully in various types of community facilities including their home, group homes, developmental centers, residential schools, hospitals, and institutions. Therefore, additional relevant competencies needed by their teachers are:

A. Knowledge of the types, advantages, and disadvantages of alternate service delivery models
B. Skill in organization
   1. Time management
   2. Scheduling
   3. Use of Space
C. Appropriate utilization of support personnel, i.e. teacher assistants, child care or residence workers.

Teachers of the visually handicapped should be able to function as an integral part of a transdisciplinary team in meeting the complex needs of MI-VH students. They will need to know and understand the roles and functions of the various disciplines including but not limited to medicine; education; social work; psychology; occupational, physical and speech therapies; and vocational rehabilitation. They must be knowledgeable in the terminologies utilized by each. Operating as part of such a team and offering limited direct and/or consultative services affords the teacher of visually handicapped students the opportunity to be both a teacher and learner as he/she demonstrates his/her expertise and, in turn benefits from the knowledge and skills of the other team members from various fields, all on behalf of MI-VH students. Additionally, the teacher of the MI-VH student will be responsible for developing in the other team members an understanding of and the techniques for meeting the unique needs of this population which are directly attributable to their visual impairment. It also affords the teacher of the visually handicapped the opportunity to be an advocate for the multi-impaired student with a visual impairment.

Also critical for such a teacher is an understanding of the needs of parents of MI-VH students as well as strategies for helping them to meet those needs. The ability to provide resources and information to parents, to serve as an advocate for and with them, to establish counseling and support mechanisms, and to train parents to assist in the development and implementation of their child's program are all facets of the teacher's role in a comprehensive parent participation program.

Although not all teachers of the visually handicapped will work with MI-VH students, those who do will need to have the additional competencies as described in this paper which would enable them to appropriately serve this population. Teacher preparation programs and school personnel responsible for the inservice training options exist. These options could include the following:

A. Specialized graduate level training programs for

teachers of deaf-blind and/or MI-VH visually handicapped children

B. Courses designed to provide information and techniques for working with MI-VH students

C. Summer inservice workshops on various topics relating to the MI-VH student, i.e. assessment, behavior management

D. Utilization of consultants from both the field of the visually handicapped and from other disciplines on a regular basis

E. Provision of ongoing after school topical workshops in areas such as vision assessment and remediation, feeding, motor development, language development, etc.

F. Opportunities for visitations to exemplary programs serving MI-VH children

G. Utilization of available inservice training packages developed to train staff working with severely handicapped students

H. Training modules specifically designed to train teachers of MI-VH students

I. Encouragement for teachers of the visually handicapped to take additional courses in other disciplines

Planning for the future offers exciting challenges and presents us with the need to change. The expansion of the roles, function, and competencies of the teacher of the visually handicapped would enable us to provide the best possible services to visually handicapped students with multi-impairments and it would guarantee that our field would remain in the forefront of special education in the years to come.

Reference
Spungin, S. Vision field must define teacher's role, function. *DVH Newsletter*, Vol. xxiv, No. 2, December 1979.

PARENT/EDUCATOR COOPERATIVE EFFORTS IN EDUCATION OF THE VISUALLY HANDICAPPED

Verna Hart, University of Pittsburgh
Kay Alicyn Ferrell, American Foundation for the Blind

Recent research findings have substantiated what teachers of handicapped children have known for years based on clinical experiences—direct involvement of parents in the education of their children results in significantly greater gains for the handicapped child. The Division for the Visually Handicapped of the Council for Exceptional Children affirms the need for the cooperative efforts of parents, children and teachers. To establish such partnerships, teachers must be commited to working with parents in arrangements where each party has distinct roles and responsibilities, and in which both are willing to exert a 100% effort to bring about an environment conducive to optimal functioning of visually handicapped children.

In order to facilitate this partnership, teachers and parents of visually handicapped children should approach the relationship with:

• Recognition that parents are their children's first and most important teachers

• Assumption that parents know their child better than anyone else

• Recognition of the permanence of parenthood and the burdens and expectations it imposes

• Recognition of the various roles parents must play including those of nurturer, teacher, advocate, case manager, and a realization that these roles cannot be assumed easily or without preparation due to the structure and complexity of today's educational laws

• Insight into the right to dislike the disability and/or its manifestations, but with a need for acceptance of the child as an individual

• Realization that teachers and parents are not in competition for the love or attention of children

• Insight into the needs of visually handicapped children without irrational expectations or fears

• Empathy for and outreach to all parents of visually handicapped children including efforts to establish active parent support groups

• Commitment to educate the public about the characteristics and needs of visually handicapped children so that similarities as well as differences in relation to normally sighted peers may be accepted

• Realization that parents and teachers have the need to interact according to their own personal styles, idiosyncracies and desires

• Mutual trust and cooperative effort

• Mutual recognition of each party's individuality and expertise

• Understanding of the necessity for an open and honest relationship

• Willingness to communicate and honestly discuss situations, particularly when there is a disagreement or a lack of understanding

• Realization that, if differences of opinion occur, those differences should be directly addressed by the persons involved rather than with anyone else

• Reciprocity in sharing information

- Openness to suggestions
- Knowledge about and utilization of all available services and resources
- Ability to make decisions based on the best information and advice currently available, and reluctance to place blame for mistakes on any one party
- Awareness that the best interests of the child always override all other considerations
- Recognition that a positive approach is important when working with children
- Reciprocity of parent/child/teacher efforts to understand behavior and behavior change
- Willingness to reinforce each other's instructional efforts for the sake of the child's learning continuity and achievement
- Awareness of children's strengths, and enjoyment of their progress
- Ability to help visually handicapped children develop and maintain self-esteem
- Understanding when making decisions that consideration must be given to the fact that visually handicapped children will grow into visually handicapped adults

- Concern for child abuse, both mental and physical, imposed at home or in school, and an agreement to seek help from appropriate sources if needed
- Recognition and appreciation of the needs of family members of the visually handicapped child so efforts can be made to balance the energy and commitment of services to meet the needs of all family members
- Commitment to legislative action for advocacy of educational rights of visually handicapped children
- Organized efforts to bring parents of visually handicapped children together to share experiences and learn from each other

For an educational program to be most effective, the parent/educator partnership should be mutually cooperative and supportive; it should have an impact beyond the immediate circle of individual participants working with the child. When actively nurtured and developed, this partnership stimulates and nurtures to the maximum extent possible the growth and development of the child with a visual impairment and facilitates the child's unique contribution to family and ultimately to society at large.

Ethical practice in the provision of services to blind and visually impaired infants, children, and youth

Kathleen Mary Huebner, Ph.D.
National Consultant on Education
Kay Alicyn Ferrell, Ph.D.
National Consultant on Early Childhood
American Foundation for the Blind

Ethics, standards of conduct, moral judgement, and philosophy are an intrinsic part of everyone's lives. A comparison of the codes of ethics of various human service professionals reveals similar categories in which inherent concepts are expressed. These categories generally include the ethics of professional competence; relationships with colleagues, students or clients, and the society at large; legal responsibilities; and employment practices (Ducanis & Golin, 1979; Heller, 1983; Welsh & Blasch, 1980). Each individual has a set of personal ethics that guides his or her behavior, but professionals who serve blind and visually impaired persons have a responsibility to commit themselves to the ethics of their profession as well.

This article addresses concepts, issues, and areas of concern that relate to professional ethics, some of which are unique to serving blind and visually impaired individuals and others that can be generalized to the practice of education. Clearly, the standards of practice discussed in this article are not all-inclusive, but are those that we, the authors, have observed or identified as being the most critical. In the first section, the issues reflect the social, economic, political, and educational climate of the 1980s, particularly as it affects the provision of services to blind and visually impaired students.

Regardless of outside influences, some aspects of professional ethics and conduct remain constant. These are addressed in the second section. This article examines legal mandates and public policy and discusses the realities of providing services, trends in the delivery of disability-specific and generic services, decisions in the neonatal intensive care unit, professional

Reprinted from *Ethical Issues in the Field of Blindness*, pp. 9-19. ©1986, American Foundation for the Blind.

accountability, responsibilities to students, and relationships with colleagues and parents.

CONTEMPORARY ETHICAL CONCERNS: LEGAL MANDATES AND PUBLIC POLICY

Background

Education in the United States became mandatory in the early part of this century primarily to advance the economic and political development of the country. Education had always been available for the children of wealthy citizens, usually in private schools and institutions of higher learning. Universal education, however, was something new and represented a commitment to a higher ideal—a way of generating common ideas, values, and basic skills in a diverse population to prepare citizens to meet the needs of the community.

Although schools for students who were blind, deaf, or mentally impaired were established, the funding mechanism was different; instead of being financed out of general school taxes, special schools and institutions were supported directly by state legislatures or through private donations. The implication was clear: these students were different. The ideals of universal education did not apply to individuals with disabilities.

The attitude toward education for children with disabilities did not change substantially during the first half of this century. Blind and visually impaired children continued to attend residential schools. They were not routinely enrolled in public schools until the mid-1950s when the number of blind and visually impaired children increased dramatically as a result of the higher incidence of retrolental fibroplasia. When these children reached mandatory school age, it was natural to assume that they would attend school in their home towns and that, given a little help, it would be possible for them to do so. Educators and parents of blind and visually impaired children worked together to assure that it would be successful.

John F. Kennedy's election in 1960 ushered in a new era of awareness of disabilities, spurred by the civil rights movement and the Kennedy family's open discussion of a member's mental retardation. Kennedy established the first President's Committee on Mental Retardation, which was followed by Congress' passage of the first laws mandating the provision of supplementary funds for public schools with special education programs. The administration of Lyndon B. Johnson continued this progress. Johnson's administration was the time of the Great Society—the belief that the government could make a better life for its citizens. Head Start, designed to prepare disadvantaged preschool children for school; and the Handicapped Children's Early Education Program, which funded model demonstration projects for infants and preschoolers, were established by Congress during that period. Almost all the legislative action affecting students with disabilities occurred at the federal level.

However, these efforts were not enough. In the early 1970s, children were still kept out of school because they had disabilities. But the political activism of the 1960s was carried over into the 1970s. Parents became more vocal in questioning why their children were not allowed to go to school or why they had to pay to send one child to a special school while other children were educated in public schools with public funds. Lawsuits were filed, and the courts decided that there was no legitimate reason why some children should be allowed to attend publicly supported schools and some should not. Children who were kept out of school were being denied the equal protection of the laws guaranteed by the Fourteenth Amendment; all children, including those with a disability, were entitled to an education at the public's expense.

Education for All Handicapped Children Act

The Education for All Handicapped Children Act (P.L. 94-142, amended and reauthorized in 1984 as P.L. 98-199), was the result of this activism. Signed by President Gerald R. Ford in 1975, it was preceded by months of public testimony that vividly demonstrated that disabled children were being denied an education; that parents were often ignored by the educational system; and that the special education programs that did exist were often provided at the convenience of the school without regard to their appropriateness for the needs of individual children.

The act and its supporting regulations are strong statements in support of

- The child's right to an education that is appropriate to his or her needs and is provided at public expense.

- The right of parents to participate in decision making in relation to their children's education.
- The child's right to be judged or evaluated fairly, according to his or her needs—not in relation to some nebulous concept of normality.
- The child's right to educational placement that fits the child, instead of fitting the child to a placement that is available.
- The right of a child with disabilities to attend a neighborhood school, if possible, and to be placed in the least restrictive environment that can meet the child's educational needs.
- The concept that learning to perform life skills, such as toileting, dressing, hygiene, and eating, is as legitimate an educational effort as learning to read, write, and do arithmetic.
- The concept that children with disabilities may need more or different services than do children without disabilities so they can benefit from the education process.

On the surface, the act guarantees that every child with a disability will receive a free, appropriate, public education. The key word is *appropriate;* the education provided must not be limited to the standard variety given to children without disabilities but should be tailored to the specific needs of the individual child. The act also recognizes that education does not mean the same thing for all children—that, for some, education may mean preparation for college, business, or blue-collar occupations, while for others, it may mean learning life-survival skills. P.L. 94-142 allows for individual rights and needs; as such, it stands proudly as the Bill or Rights for students with disabilities.

The reality of providing services

There is a difference between what a law stands for and how it is applied. There would be no need for the massive body of special education regulations if agencies and individuals acted in the spirit that the law intended. Unfortunately, individuals interpret the law in different ways. The federal regulations implementing the Education for All Handicapped Children Act have spawned separate sets of regulations in every state and local education agency. Thus, there is little uniformity in how the law is applied or interpreted and no guarantee that funds will be available to implement the regulations. The following are some examples:

- Blind children in one state automatically attend a residential school while those in a neighboring state automatically attend a public school.

- One student receives orientation and mobility training while another with equal needs does not.
- Low-vision examinations are standard practice in some states, required by state statute; optional in some states; and unheard of in others.
- Parents are invited to attend Individualized Educational Program (IEP) meetings and are handed a completed form to sign, instead of being involved in the planning and writing of the IEP for their children.
- Schools frequently attempt to provide the minimum number of services possible. Parents of blind and visually impaired children must depend on other parents and supportive professionals to tell them what is available and what is possible educationally. They are forced to be aggressive in seeking answers in a system that encourages an adversarial relationship.
- Students are routinely found eligible for a specific class placement before the IEP is written.
- Resource rooms have become self-contained classrooms for visually impaired students instead of the short-term resource centers they were designed to be.
- Parents and children are offered the type of program that the school has available instead of the type of program that best meets their needs.

Instead of doing everything possible to assure an appropriate, individualized education for blind and visually impaired children, local and state education agencies often view the children's needs and rights as an imposition and offer as little as possible. Instead of changing to meet the needs of children with disabilities, schools expect the children to fit into the mold of available programs. Eleven years after P.L. 94-142 was signed into law, and nine years after it went into effect, children with disabilities are still outsiders—are still knocking on the door asking to come in.

Issues of compliance

Frequently, legislators create good laws but fail to look beyond the immediate concern they sought to assuage. The Education for All Handicapped Children Act is an exception; provisions were made at the time of passage for monitoring and gradually increasing the levels of funding. Unfortunately, the present political and economic climate has brought into question the ability to fulfill the original intent. However, even this act did not expect that

- "Least restrictive environment" would be interpreted as the neighborhood school and that the possibility that the school might be more restrictive than an institution for some children would be ignored.
- Visually impaired children would attend neighborhood

schools but not receive their books and materials in accessible media or their instruction from a professional who could help them learn to use these media.
- Students who had been routinely sent to residential schools and institutions would attend neighborhood schools before the community schools were prepared for their entrance and that severely disabled students would be discharged from institutions without adequate preparation into communities that were not ready to accept them.

Unduplicated counts

Approximately 30-50 percent of all blind and visually impaired children have one or more additional disabilities (Kirchner, 1983; Packer & Kirchner, in press). The child-count provisions of P.L. 94-142 require that children be classified only in one category of impairment. Funding formulas are attached by state education agencies to those categories, often according to arbitrary comparisons of costs attributable to the various disabling conditions. This practice may encourage local education agencies to count children according to the disability that will return the most money or to the programs and personnel they have available or are willing to pay for. Children who are blind and have cerebral palsy, for example, may be counted in the multiply handicapped category because they spend much of their time with teachers and therapists who address their motor needs. These children and their teachers may also receive instruction and consultation from a teacher of the visually impaired; but, for all practical purposes, that time does not count toward funding. The requirement of an unduplicated count forces local and state agencies to reduce a primary and critical learning need to the level of an ancillary service.

The importance of accurate counts should not be taken lightly. Besides their use in funding formulas, these counts are utilized for documenting the state of the art, analyzing trends in services, projecting the need for teachers, and planning for a continuum of educational placements at the state and local levels. According to the U.S. Department of Education (1984), the population of visually impaired children decreased from 1978 to 1982. This decline may have been a result of the unduplicated count; multiply handicapped visually impaired students were classified as only multiply handicapped and hence as not needing the services of teachers of the visually impaired, regardless of whether they were receiving those services. Because fewer visually impaired children were identified, it was assumed that fewer teachers of visually impaired children would be needed in later years. If provision had been made to account for the amount of service given by teachers of the blind and visually impaired to students counted in other categories, there might not be as many vacant teaching positons as there are today.

Another problem may become evident in the years ahead as a result of the unduplicated count. Today's infants and preshool children have different etiologies and educational needs than does the current school-age population; if the state education agencies rely only on the unduplicated count figures, they may be unprepared for tomorrow's blind and visually impaired students. Comprehensive demographic studies, separate from the child-count provisions of the current law, must be conducted on a national basis if future needs are to be met.

A visual impairment in and of itself affects the way in which a child obtains information about the world. This fact alone requires professionals who are trained in specific and unique methodologies to be primary deliverers of services to visually impaired children. Local education agencies must be encouraged and supported in their efforts to count blind and visually impaired children both as a distinct group and as part of other handicapped groups when these children are or should be receiving the services of professionals trained to work with blind and visually impaired children.

Appropriation of funds

Congress has yet to appropriate funds at the level it stipulated in 1975. One strength of the act was built-in incentives for local education agencies to implement the law—its provision for distributing federal funds to state agencies at a rate of 40 percent of the excess cost of educating a disabled child. But even the remainder is difficult for some local education agencies to assume, and in fiscal year 1985, the federal appropriations for educating children with disabilities were only 1 percent of the total excess cost of special education. It is difficult enough to legislate morality; it is harder when legislators do not keep their promises and citizens remain apathetic. Professionals should continue to press Congress to appropriate funds at a level that permits the full implementation of the law.

Monitoring mechanisms

Mechanisms for monitoring compliance with the law are extensive but have little enforcement power. In the first few years after the law was passed, the Bureau of Education for the Handicapped (now the U.S. Department of Educa-

tion, Office of Special Education Programs) sent out teams to monitor the state agencies' compliance with the basic provisions of the federal law. The state agencies, in turn, monitored the local education agencies. Today, the compliance with federal law is measured by little more than the collection of data and the examination of state plans. IEPs of visually impaired children are not regularly reviewed by individuals with appropriate expertise, and parents and students are not consulted during the process. Eleven years after the passage of P.L. 94-142, 21 states are still deficient in the development of IEPs; 18 states do not make available a continuum of alternative placements; and 16 states do not guarantee a free, appropriate, public education to all children (U.S. Department of Education, 1984).

It is reasonable to question why an elaborate set of regulations exists when infractions are uncorrected, monitoring procedures are weak, and funds have yet to be withheld for noncompliance. Professionals and professional organizations have a responsibility not only to report noncompliance, but to initiate and pursue fair hearings on behalf fo unserved, underserved, and inappropriately served visually impaired students.

Response to the National Commission study

In 1983, a study commissioned by the Department of Education, entitled *a Nation at Risk* (National Commission on Excellence in Education, 1983), documented deficiencies in the American educational system and called for widespread educational reform in such areas as the preparation of teachers, achievement by students, basic skills, and course offerings. The study has generated considerable controversy, several additional reports, and proposals for reform that may have an adverse impact on the field of special education.

Merit raises and the promotion of teachers

The study has prompted efforts to make salary raises for and the promotion of teachers contingent on the teachers' merits, as demonstrated by the achievement of students. These efforts may have an unfair impact on teachers of students with all types of handicaps. The proposal is faulty; it rests on the *mean* performance of all students, which implies that some students achieve above the mean and others achieve below the mean. It also implies that teachers are sucessful in teaching some students but not all students. This implication seems to contradict the rationale behind the proposal and would result in some children achieving and others not. Teachers of children with disabilities might unconsciously lower their expectations for their students and adjust the IEPs downward in an attempt to place their students' achievement in the best possible light.

Proposals for merit raises for teachers also reduce the educational process to the "survival of the fittest," whereby those who are most likely to succeed will be helped to do so and those who are least likely to succeed will be least helped. If that is the case, it is difficult to see how this particular educational reform is any different from the status quo. Efforts to make the promotion of teachers and salary increases contingent on the achievement of students must be exposed as being contrary to legitimate educational reform and ethical practice.

Equal opportunities

The same opportunities for academic, career-vocational, social, and technological endeavors that are available to regular education students must be afforded to blind and visually impaired students. However, blind and visually impaired students need more time to accomplish many academic and daily living tasks and for taking tests. In addition to a standard curriculum, these students need to receive instruction in areas that are unique to visual impairment, such as literary braille, the Nemeth code, abacus, orientation and mobility, the development of concepts, sensory training, the utilization of low vision, listening skills, and the use of technological devices such as Optacon, paperless braillers, and computer accessibility, equipment, and strategies. Yet students continue to be expected to carry a standard curriculum; learn a cadre of special skills; participate in social, extracurricular, and prevocational activities; and complete elementary and secondary education in the same time as their sighted peers.

This expectation creates pressures on teachers to treat certain aspects of their students' programs as priorities. As a result, students either do not receive instruction in all areas or they receive minimal instruction in some areas. The areas that are neglected vary, depending on the instructors', administrators', parents', and students' intuitively set priorities. Clearly, the ethics of such a practice must be questioned. Professionals have an ethical responsibiltiy to consider each child's educational process holistically and to assure a balance among the opportunities for cognitive, social, emotional, and vocational development.

Extracurricular activities

Many administrators and boards of education have instituted policies that make participation in extracurricular activities contingent on a student's achievement of a minimal grade average. Such policies view participation in athletics and clubs as perquisites that are unrelated to the educational process. However, extracurricular activities are critical elements in the socialization, character building, and leadership training of students and help to develop a team spirit and good work habits. Furthermore, these activities are supported by public education funds and staffed by teachers and others under contract to the school system. Students with disabilities have only recently been allowed comparable access to extracurricular activities.

Nonparticipation in sports or other extracurricular activities does not necessarily cause students to pay greater attention to academic pursuits. It may instead result in decreased self-esteem because a student's overall perception of his or her succes may be lower. The impact may be even greater on students with disabilities, whose participation is frequently limited by the nature of the disability or by a reluctance to take risks. Since the proportion of visually impaired students is low in relation to the entire school population and teachers and supervisors may be inexperienced in accommodating them, visually impaired youngsters are more likely to be misunderstood and to underachieve than are the regular education students. Therefore, restrictions on extracurricular activities may fall particularly hard on them. Without a proper understanding of the needs of visually impaired students, adaptations and critical services may not be provided in sufficient quantity or quality to allow the students to achieve in the regular school setting. The increased social and emotional experiences gained by participation in extracurricular activities may thus be denied to students who need them as much as, if not more than, their sighted peers. Efforts to limit visually impaired students' participation in extracurricular activities must be defeated.

Special certificates

High school diplomas are awarded at the completion of a course of study that includes prerequisites in English, history, mathematics, science, and physical education. The possession of a diploma signals to employers and institutions of higher learning that a student has received a basic education and has skills that are comparable to those held by the general population of high school graduates.

Students with disabilities may attend school until they have reached the maximum mandatory school age but never complete the state-required course of study for a high school diploma. Such students receive no diploma and possibly no acknowledgement of achievement to mark a milestone in their lives. Many school districts are now awarding certificates of completion for students who do not follow the usual secondary curriculum. Local public schools should establish cerificates of completion that recognize the achievement of students with disabilities and their movement into another stage of life.

Blind and visually impaired students with no other handicapping conditions who receive appropriate services that are unique to their needs by qualified personnel should have little difficulty in fulfilling their state's requirements for a high school diploma. Therefore, no special certificate program is needed for visually impaired students with no other disability. Visually impaired students who are cognitively impaired or who have additional handicapping conditions that affect their learning may need to be considered for a special certificate program. However, those special certificates should be available to them through the provisions made to students with other handicapping conditions.

Caution should be taken to assure that visually impaired students are not given too much leeway; in an effort to be fair to visually impaired students in homework or testing situations, the line between accommodation and indulgence sometimes is blurred. Teachers and parents are not doing visually impaired students a service by certifying that they have achieved a certain standard if they have not done so. Teachers and parents are responsible for ascertaining that visually impaired students have fairly achieved the necessary prerequisites for promotion or graduation.

Disability-specific vs. generic services

Whether services should be delivered on a generic or disability-specific basis is another current policy issue. Although the federal government has not yet mandated a generic approach, it has set a trend and encouraged such an approach by limiting its support to programs that address generic rather than disability-specific services. For example, P.L. 98-199 is "intended to support services [through grants] to parents of a full range of handicapped children, not services relating to one category of children" (Division of Educational Services, 1984, p. 16). Applications have been rejected when the expressed needs were limited to parents of children in one or a few categories. Although professionals may be involved in the preparation of applications and the proposed projects, parents are to be the primary participants.

Parents who have children with low-incidence dis-abilities need the support of self-help groups of parents with similar experiences. Although some areas of need are common to parents regardless of their child's disability, others are disability specific. For example, parents of blind children will benefit from specific training in the techniques of eating, orientation and mobility, Optacon and Versabraille use, and other skills that are unique to children who are blind. A qualifier such as "support services to parents of a full range of handicapped children" (Division of Educational Services, 1984, p.16) requires parents to extend themselves to involve groups of parents whose children have other disabilities, develop training programs that will be relevant to children with multiple disablilities, and, if funded, attend training sessions in which they will have to wade through the content to determine "what" is applicable to their children. In addition, they may not even have the opportunity for receiving or sharing disability-specific information that is critical to supporting themselves, each other, and their blind or visually impaired children.

State after state has adopted a generic model and thus has eliminated disability-specific state consultants. Such policies place parents, regular and special education teachers, related service providers, administrators, legislators, and other concerned citizens at a critical disadvantage. They raise questions such as these:

1. To whom can one turn for the following types of expertise?
   - Information about available state services.
   - Referral to appropriate schools and agencies.
   - The identification of parent, support, and advocacy groups.
   - Consultation on "appropriate" services for students.
   - Information on state and federal laws regarding the education of visually impaired students.
   - Information about the availability and location of materials.
   - Assistance in specialized techniques that are unique to blind and visually impaired students.
2. Who at the state level will be qualified to assume the responsibility for
   - Coordinating state special projects related to blindness and visual impairment.
   - Developing in-service training programs for teachers of visually impaired children and mainstream teachers who have blind and visually impaired students in their class.
   - Supervising and monitoring vision programs.
   - Providing research data and other types of information on blind and visually impaired students.

- Representing a state's vision services at national, state, regional, and local meetings, conferences, and workshops.

Who, in states that adopt the generic model, will be qualified and responsible for the provision of appropriate and high quality services for visually impaired students? Who, at the state level, will understand the unique needs of visually impaired infants, children, and youth; disseminate the information to those who need and request it, and assure that appropiate services are provided to the children and their families?

Eleven years after the passage of P.L. 94-142, there are blind and visually impaired students who are

- Receiving no special services unique to their visual impairment. Do these students have a chance to attain their maximum potiential?

- Placed in resource rooms, preschool classrooms, and other programs designed for learning-disabled, developmentally delayed, emotionally disturbed, deaf and hearing impaired students, or some combination thereof, although the visually impaired students have none of these disabling conditions. Think of the academic, social, emotional, and psychological effects of such inappropriate placements. Why do parents have to go through due process hearings to correct such placements?

- Instructed by teachers who are certified in generic special education or mildly or severely profound handicapping conditions but who have little or no foundation in teaching blind and visually impaired youngsters. How can these students receive an appropriate education? Are these teachers knowledgeable in the techniques and strategies that most effectively promote the conceptual development that blind and visually impaired students need to transfer what they have learned to new situations? Are they familiar with and experienced in special subject areas that are unique to students with visual impairments?

- Assessed by teachers, school psychologists, and other personnel who are ignorant of the effects of a visual impairment on learning, concept development, motor development, and the like and who therefore make inaccurate findings and placements. For example, blind students who exhibit echolalia may be falsely labeled as mentally retarded. Will these students realize their potential, if teachers' and parents' expectations are lowered as a result of invalid assessments completed by unqualified personnel?

- Placed in inappropriate programs by school-district supervisors who have no expertise in the education of blind and visually impaired children or who rely on a computerized IEP or one that has been completed by someone other than a qualified teacher of visually impaired children. How can such IEPs be valid or fulfill the intent of the law?

- Provided with an aide, generally well intended, sometimes with a high school diploma, who is assigned to "help" students in lieu of specialized education services by a teacher of the visually impaired. Is an aide who is assigned to read to the student, write in examination responses, take the student from class to class, and carry cafeteria trays for the student helping to teach independence? How can such assistance be construed as appropriate education? Is it not a paternalistic approach that fosters dependence?

- Residing in rural areas without any vision services and therefore continue to be placed in residential schools, hundreds of miles from their homes. The residential schools may indeed be providing an appropriate education, but is such practice in compliance with federal mandates? What are the alternatives? Have all service delivery options been exhausted?

- Receiving specialized instruction in areas unique to blindness, such as braille, abacus, and Nemeth code, by rehabilitation counselors and rehabilitation teachers who lack the appropriate degrees and knowledge of child development, pedagogy and methods and strategies for assessment, the development of objectives, lesson plans, and evaluation. Certainly, state and private rehabilitation agencies are to be credited for recognizing the needs of unserved students, but are unqualified personnel providing the most appropriate services as mandated?

It is only with educational services that address the unique needs of blind and visually impaired infants, children, and youth and that are provided by qualified personnel that students will be afforded their right to an appropriate education and will be competent to take their rightful place in society. To end blatant injustices that result from inappropriate generic services is an ethical responsibility. It requires professionals, parents, and other concerned citizens to be vocal and active advocates for blind and visually impaired students and their families. It means that parents must be informed about their children's rights and supported in defending these rights. It means that sometimes the system must be challenged.

Moreover, to ensure the rights of all blind and visually impaired infants, children, and youth, professionals must do more than react to crises; they must become proactive. The unique needs of blind and visually impaired students must be understood by *all* service providers—including regular education teachers, administrators, and legislators. Advocates for blind and visually impaired children must encourage and facilitate this understanding. If they are successful, professionals and parents will no longer have to explain and defend the rights of blind and visually impaired students, and high-quality educational services will be a reality for all blind and visually impaired infants, children, and youth.

Decisions in the neonatal intensive care nursery

Public attention in recent years has focused on the federal government's efforts to monitor the treatment of handicapped infants in neonatal intensive care units (NICUs). Although euthanasia has been practiced without public notice for many years (Duff & Campbell, 1973), the publicity surrounding the choices made by two families in two different hospitals brought the ethical questions to the fore. In both cases, the infants had birth defects that were surgically correctable.

The parents of one infant, born with Down syndrome and esophageal atresia, refused, on the advice of one physician but contrary to the advice of another, permission to operate to repair the esophagus so the child could eat. The infant starved to death. In the second case, an infant born with myelomeningocele, hydrocephalus, and microcephaly, was denied surgery to close her back and drain fluid from the brain. Again, medical personnel were divided on the course of treatment, and the infant's parents declined permission to operate. The hospital was taken to court by the U.S. Department of Health and Human Services in an attempt to force the hospital to provide treatment under Section 504 of the Rehabilitation Act of 1973, which prohibits discrimination against individuals with handicaps. The courts did not order treatment. This child is still alive; the myelomeningocele healed naturally, and the parents eventually gave permission for other previously denied surgery.

There are many issues involving the right to treatment for infants with disabilities. Questions abound about how decisions are made, who makes them, and when. On cursory examination, those who are concerned with providing services to blind and visually impaired persons might not think that day-to-day occurrences in the neonatal intensive care unit have an impact on their work. The fact is that 30-50 percent of the infants who weigh less than 1,000 grams (2.2 pounds) at birth become handicapped, 15-30 percent of them severely (Lyon, 1985). It has been estimated that one-third to one-half of the identified population of visually impaired

children is multiply handicapped (Packer & Kirchner, in press) and that the vast number of multiply handicapped children has never received an ophthalmological examination or functional vision evaluation by a qualified professional. Therefore, the likelihood that treatment decisions made in the neonatal intensive care nursery will affect visually impaired infants and their families and thus the professionals who serve them is much greater than it might appear.

Consider the following situations:

- Parents of a preterm, low-birthweight infant with respiratory distress syndrome were informed that the treatment options lead to their child becoming blind or brain damaged.

- A child, who as an infant was diagnosed as blind by a pediatric ophthalmologist, was assessed at 18 months by a teacher of the visually impaired using new psycho-educational techniques as having a visual acuity of 20/450. When the child was 4 years old, the ophthalmologist confirmed the educator's findings with a visual acuity measured at 20/400.

- A child with a flat visual evoked potential at 12 months, treated as a blind child until his teacher observed him picking up a raisin on a brown rug, was reading large print in first grade.

- A severely handicapped teenager, institutionalized since birth, was observed laughing appropriately at a staff member's jokes. Subsequent psychological testing and training with a language board revealed unsuspected cognitive ability.

- It has been estimated that one-third of the Down syndrome population also has a visual impairment. At least one study has found that the average IQ of school-age children with Down syndrome who have participated in early intervention programs is 79, which is within normal limits. Some children in the study had to have had IQs well within the normal limits for such a high mean to have resulted with a population generally considered to function with IQs of 70 and below.

- A 30-week gestational-age infant remained in the NICU for 12 months, unable to be weaned from oxygen. On the basis of visual development research, the bright, highly reflective, low-contrast environment of the NICU offered little stimulus to the infant to use her developing vision. When finally discharged, the child was functionally blind.

- A child born at term with bilateral anophthalmia was placed in an NICU for several weeks and received routine care.

- In a leading tertiary care facility, the social work staff does not believe in referring families to services for blind and visually impaired infants until the parents have "bonded" to their babies.

- A preterm infant had respiratory distress syndrome and patent ductus arteriosus and subsequently developed retinopathy of prematurity. Twice, he experienced respiratory arrest and was resuscitated; he died at 16 months.
- Parents were advised to institutionalize their baby, who had rubella. They did so temporarily, then took him home because of dissatisfaction with his treatment and education. Today that child is a photographer at a major entertainment complex in the South.
- Another family of a child who had rubella lived outside the catchment area for services. At age 18, the young man ate independently but was neither toilet trained nor able to dress himself. The only way his parents knew how to manage his frequent outbursts of behavior was by locking him in his sparsely furnished bedroom. The local general practitioner did not allow the adolescent in his office or waiting room but examined him in the car. Under anesthesia in the hospital, an ophthalmologist discovered that the boy's eyeball had shriveled to the size of a pea and had probably been the cause of severe pain.
- The American Foundation for the Blind has been asked to provide information to lawyers representing plaintiffs in wrongful life suits against physicians who have saved infants' lives but not prevented blindness or severe handicapping conditions.

All professionals who provide services to visually impaired persons are aware of similar events. The foregoing examples alone provide sufficient reason to be concerned about occurrences in the NICU because they illustrate that medical and other health care professionals are making decisions or advising parents on the basis of (1) misinformation about the child's potential, (2) ignorance about recent advances in early intervention, education, and technology, and (3) disinterest in referring families to community service organizations. As the examples showed, it is difficult to predict during infancy the degree of visual impairment an individual will have at school age or older. Diagnoses of total blindness made in the NICU have often proved to be less than absolute. Therefore, predictions of near or total blindness made during the neonatal period are suspect and should never play a part in decisions of whether to treat other medical complications. Furthermore, physicians and other hospital personnel are not immune to the stereotypical view of blind persons as dependent and

dysfunctional citizens. At a time when medical personnel have an extraordinary influence, they should not be allowed to prejudice parents.

In an attempt to deal with preconceived notions of the quality of life of individuals with disabilities, Congress passed the Child Abuse Amendments of 1984 (P.L. 98-457). To receive grants under the Child Abuse Prevention and Treatment Act, states must "establish programs and/or procedures within the State's child protective service system to respond to reports of medical neglect, including reports of the withholding of medically indicated treatment for disabled infants with life-threatening conditions" (*Federal Register,* 49 [238], 48160). The act provides for the establishment of Infant Care Review Committees (ICRCs) at hospitals to develop policies and guidelines for treating infants with handicapping conditions and to act as resources to hospital personnel and families on current information about the medical treatment of handicapped infants. All cases involving the treatment of handicapped infants are to be reviewed by the ICRCs, which are made up of a practicing physician, a nurse, a social worker, an advocate from a handicapped group, and a member of the hospital's medical staff. Committees are encouraged to add a member of the clergy. It is significant to note that neither the parents of the infant under consideration (on an ad hoc basis) nor a special educator are required or even recommended to be on the ICRCs. There is no stipulation that the advocate be from a group representing the same disability as the infant under review. ICRC committees should include members with training and experience in the educational, vocational, and independent-living capabilities of the specific disability group to which the infant under review belongs.

The field of blindness has an ethical responsibility to endorse the "Principles of Treatment of Disabled Infants," appended to this article. It is suggested further that the ethical decision extends beyond the NICU to include life after discharge. Sustaining life without acknowledging the right to a myriad of education, social, financial, psychological, and medical services to support that life and the fulfillment of its potential is unrealistic and cruel. Sustaining life without providing those services and the funds to implement them is unconscionable. It becomes little more than triage in the nursery.

The true ethical dilemma for professionals is this: Whether to fight for the right of blind and visually impaired infants to receive high-quality services that address their unique needs or to be content with the erosion of services in all areas of service delivery and social policy. Professionals who provide services to visually impaired persons have no other choice but to do the following:

- Aggressively advocate for state and federal legislation that mandates comprehensive services for visually impaired infants from birth to 3 years.
- Infuse their discipline into the medical community 1) attending medical conferences, 2) providing written materials to physicians and other health care professionals, 3) speaking at hospital grand rounds on current educational, vocational, and independent living perspectives for visually impaired children, and 4) regularly visiting neonatal intensive care units and leaving literature for parents urging them to seek appointment to ICRCs.

ETHICAL CONSTANTS

Professional accountability

Professionals have an obligation to strive constantly and actively toward excellence in the services they provide to students and their families. It is important that they recognize their strengths, weaknesses, and limitations. They must apply and share these strengths; acknowledge and remediate their weaknesses through continuing education, both formal and informal; and reach out to others who can provide needed services that are beyond their capacity.

Personnel preparation

It is during college and university training that the foundations of knowledge, theory, methodology, and best practice are laid, and it is during the years of actual teaching experience that knowledge is expanded, theory and methodology are implemented, and skills are refined. Personnel preparation programs have a formidable job and an exciting challenge. The population of students is heterogeneous, and the needs of students are ever changing. Today's teachers work with blind and visually impaired youngsters of all ages, with a complexity of additional disabling conditions and a full range of cognitive abilities.

To expect personnel preparation programs to prepare teachers completely to work with students with every possible combination of abilities and disabilities is unreasonable and unrealistic. But teachers can and must be prepared to work effectively as team members, consultants, and team leaders and develop skills to work cooperatively with others involved in the total well-being of students. A solid education foundation can at best be

a framework on which teachers must build throughout their careers.

Personnel preparation programs must continuously assess the needs of blind and visually impaired students and their families and be responsive to them by updating and modifying the content of their programs. Professionals who are responsible for pre- and in-service training programs have an ethical responsibility to expand their knowledge and skills. They have an obligation to incorporate valid research findings and to introduce new information, innovative techniques, and model programs into the courses they teach.

Today, personnel preparation programs face a critical problem: the recruitment of potential teachers and orientation and mobility instructors for blind and visually impaired infants, children, and youth. Young people are more interested in pursuing careers in business and industry than they are in human service occupations. Therefore, the country is facing a critical shortage of teachers. The federal government, particularly the Reagan administration, has addressed the need for science and mathematics teachers. It has not addressed the overwhelming need for teachers of exceptional children, especially of blind and visually impaired children. Rather, it has decreased its support for preparation programs for teachers of the blind and for aid to students at the bachelor's, master's, and doctoral levels. The result is not only a decline in the ability of these programs to compete with other programs, but the termination of programs. These facts cannot and should not be ignored. Complacency will lead to fewer appropriate educational services for blind and visually impaired students.

Personnel preparation programs are actively involved in recruitment efforts—a new role for which they are unprepared. Furthermore, as some college and university professors have admitted, the quality of incoming college and university students into teacher preparation programs is lower than it was in the past. Therefore, these programs are being forced to offer remedial course work in an attempt to continue to prepare qualified teachers with the necessary competencies. Until teachers gain the same respect, prestige, and financial remuneration as do other professionals, there will continue to be a severe shortage of teachers. All professionals in the field of blindness have an ethical responsibility to recognize the problem of recruiting and retaining teachers. They should take every opportunity to recruit high-quality teachers and to improve working conditions, benefits, and financial equity. Teacher preparation personnel cannot and should not bear this responsibility alone.

Standards for certification

Professionals who are concerned with competence must address the need for and enforcement of standards. From state to state, the requirements of certification and licensure vary in the area of blindness and visual impairments. Some states have no certification requirements, while others have stringent requirements for academic degrees and field experience that are specific to the disability. All committed professionals have an obligation to ensure not only that high nationwide standards are developed but that the standards are monitored and enforced. Why should a child in one state have a highly qualified and skilled teacher of the visually impaired while a child in a neighboring state has a teacher who had neither the course work nor the experience relevant to the unique needs of visually impaired learners? Can committed professionals continue to be passive when students are instructed by unqualified individuals in skill areas that are unique to their visual impairment?

Responsibilities to students

The ultimate goal and ethical responsibility of professionals who are committed to providing appropriate and high-quality education to blind and visually impaired infants, children, and youth is to facilitate the students' acquisition of the knowledge and skills that will enable them to reach their highest level of independence and to make choices. High yet realistic expectations for the students' educational, emotional, psychological, and social achievements must be based on valid assessments.

Assessment

Assessment instruments and procedures must not be utilized in such a way that they discriminate against visually impaired students because of race; color; creed; sex; age; national origin; social, economic, or family background; or nonvisual experience. When there are no valid standardized tests normed on a sample of visually impaired students, modifications must be made to take into consideration the impact of nonvisual experiences on visually impaired students' performance on tests.

Professionals must guard against developing goals for students that are based on generalizations, rumor, or intuition. To be objective, fair, and helpful, it is imperative that professionals be skilled in evaluating formal and informal assessments that have been completed by others, in conducting assessments of students, and in applying valid assessment information to the development and implementation of IEPs.

Psychologists, occupational and physical therapists, and regular education, medical, and other related service personnel most often lack knowledge of and training in the effects of blindness and visual impairment on cognitive, psychological, motor, and other areas of development. Therefore, it is the responsibility of teachers of visually impaired students to work with others who conduct such assessments to increase the validity of their procedures, findings, and recommendations. It is also the teachers' responsibility to encourage the inclusion into the pre-and in-service training programs of coursework in related fields that is relevant to visually impaired youngsters.

Supervision

Teachers of visually impaired students are frequently supervised by administrators with little or no formal training or experience in the field of blindness. This creates several problems:

- Supervisors are not aware of the techniques and methodologies used to instruct visually impaired students.
- Supervisors may question the amount of time devoted to travel, the acquisition of materials, the preparation of lesson plans, and individualized instruction.
- Teachers have a greater burden of justifying the needs of their students and the use of their time.
- IEP meetings for multiply handicapped/visually impaired students are often staffed by supervisors who have been trained in other disciplines instead of teachers of the visually impaired. Thus, the question arises of whether the meeting, as well as its outcome, is legally constituted. The law requires that IEP meetings be staffed by individuals who are knowledgeable about the student's disability.

A supervisory position implies neither knowledge nor competence. State certification standards should require that supervisors take course work in the disabilities for which they are responsible.

Advocacy

It is crucial that professionals in the field of blindness recognize inappropriate placements and educational programs, be able to substantiate why they are inappropriate, and initiate and effect changes as needed. They have an ethical responsibility to students to be skilled in acquiring the educational and support services that the students need.

Not only must professionals be aware of and enforce the educational rights of students as mandated by law, but they must inform students and their families of their rights and all potential services related to education. These rights and services include those mandated under specific laws, such as P.L. 94-142, P.L. 89-313, P.L. 98-199, and P.L. 93-380 (Family Educational Rights and Privacy Act), as well as those that are recommended, such as genetic counseling and other related services. Professionals must recognize when laws are unjust and when laws are needed to protect students' rights. For example, only 12 states require special education services from birth for visually impaired infants. Therefore, action must be taken to influence the necessary legislative changes. In addition, professionals must prepare students and their families to be their own advocates. The job of professionals is not to make students dependent, but to teach them to take charge of their lives—to be as self-sufficient, responsible, and independent as possible.

Furthermore, professionals have an ethical responsibility to be cognizant of laws pertaining to child abuse or neglect, to be familiar with procedures to follow when they suspect that a child is being abused or neglected, and to take action to ensure the physical, emotional, and psychological well-being of students.

Research

There is a paucity of scientific research on education of blind and visually impaired infants, children, and youth. Therefore, it is an ethical responsibility to be cautious in applying methodological approaches in the absence of theory, to cooperate with research efforts, to apply valid research findings to improve practice, and to disseminate practice methodologies that have a solid foundation in research. Professionals who are involved in research have a responsibility to ensure the welfare of students and families who serve as subjects by conducting research in an ethical manner, enforcing the principle of informed consent, and upholding the students' and families' rights to confidentiality. Information about students and their families should be released under specific conditions of written consent and statutory confidentiality.

Cultural considerations

It is imperative that professionals learn about and become sensitive to the cultures and customs of students and their families, treat the students and their parents with dignity, and respect their cultural preferences. Professionals should not impose their personal mores on children from different, conflicting cultures. For example, in teaching social and communication skills to American blind and visually impaired youngsters, eye contact is encouraged and reinforced. In Asian societies, eye contact is considered disrespectful.

Relationships with colleagues

The year 1984 was significant in the field of blindness, because it marked the alliance of two major professional organizations—the American Association of Workers for the Blind and the Association for Education for the Visually Handicapped. The Association for Education and Rehabilitation of the Blind and Visually Impaired is an overt demonstration of commitment by those concerned with providing high quality services to blind and visually impaired infants, children, youth, and adults, to learn from and work with each other. This alliance is a living expression of the belief that higher quality and more unified services can be provided through cooperative efforts. But membership alone in a professional organization is not sufficient to assure cooperation. A firm ethical foundation must guide each individual's commitment to working with colleagues in all related professions as well as with those from the field of blindness.

Today's teachers, orientation and mobility specialists, administrators, and support staff in special education of blind and visually impaired children are involved in providing services to more infants, preschoolers, and developmentally delayed, autistic, multiply handicapped, and perhaps identified gifted visually impaired youngsters than ever before. Therefore, they must initiate, encourage, and affirm synergistic relationships with colleagues from other areas of special education and related fields to meet both the complex needs of the children and the increased demands on those who serve them.

Ethical relationships with colleagues require professionals to do the following:
- Initiate constructive dialogue and be available and responsive to those who serve students and their families.
- Communicate effectively with others in a timely manner. Acknowledge the expertise of colleagues.
- Constructively inform colleagues of the unique needs of visually impaired students.
- Work effectively as team members or leaders, disregarding territoriality and releasing role responsibilities when necessary.
- Sublimate emotions toward colleagues for the benefit of students.
- Support and actively participate in all relevant professional organizations, including those beyond the field of blindness.

- Refer students and families to appropriate service agencies and organizations.
- Report unethical or incompetent behavior and practices to the appropriate enforcement agency.

Professionals should support their employing agencies and institutions. However, they also have an ethical responsibility to change observed injustices or conditions that are harmful to students—no matter how difficult the reporting of unethical or incompetent behavior and practices may be. The welfare of students must be the foremost consideration. This objective must guide communication and actions with professional colleagues and personnel in all types of organizations and agencies.

Responsibilities to parents

Until the mid-1970s, the involvement of parents in education—particularly in special education—was marked by a laissez-faire attitude by parents and school personnel. Parents may have participated in parent-teacher organizations and attended open house at the schools, but they generally were not involved in educational decisions for their children unless there was a problem that necessitated special consultation. In contrast to the early days of public education in this country—when parents were both the administrators and the supervisors of local schools—school officials had come to expect parents to give up their responsibilities for their children's education when the children entered the public school system.

Today, special education laws contain a number of provisions that are designed to formalize the relationship between parents of children with disabilities and the school system. Some of these provisions are as follows:
- Notification of and request to evaluate students.
- Requirements that written communications be in the parent's native language.
- Mutual involvement in the development and writing of IEPs.
- Notice of rights to due process and confidentiality.
- Mechanisms to question and appeal, if necessary, the components of IEPs.
- Representation of parents on local advisory committees.
- Participation of parents in the evaluation of programs.
- Federal grants to parent-training and information centers.

Unfortunately, these provisions have not succeeded in changing fundamentally the way parents are treated in the educational system. One study found that most discussions at IEP meetings occurred among teachers and administrators (Goldstein, Stickland, Turnbull, & Curry, 1980). The National Committee for Citizens in Education's 1979 survey of parents in 46 states found that IEPs were written by teachers and presented to parents to sign in over half the IEP meetings surveyed ("Parent Involvement," 1980). (A notice of proposed rule making initiated by the Carter Administration in 1981 attempted to clarify what may have been a legitimate effort to streamline the IEP process by emphasizing that IEPs were to be written at the IEP meeting by the entire team; the proposed rule was withdrawn by then Secretary of Education Bell before it was scheduled to take effect.) A review of printed materials used by state and local education agencies to inform parents of the law (Roit & Pfohl, 1984) concluded that the materials may not be comprehensible to a large number of families, based on the reading level of the materials and the literacy level of the U.S. population.

A study conducted by the California State Department of Education (Lynch, 1981) demonstrated that misunderstandings continue to plague parent-professional relationships. Special education teachers thought that the parents' apathy; their lack of time, energy, and understanding; and the school's not valuing the input of parents were the greatest barriers to participation of lower socioeconomic families. The teachers in this study were only doing what they had learned to do best: To judge parents, based on their own perceptions of what parents should or should not do. The parents in the study identified the greatest difficulties as logistical problems (for example, transportation and being released from work), the school system's lack of understanding, feelings of inferiority, and uncertainty about the child's disability and how the child could be helped by parents or by the school system.

This concept of judgment is not new, and is not limited to parents of children with disabilities. Teacher preparation programs are built on a strong foundation of psychoeducational theory, and it is neither uncommon nor necessarily valid to attribute the cause of a child's positive or negative behavior or learning problems to the home environment. The problem occurs when the cause is automatically attributed to the parents and family without considering other possible reasons, such as the deterioration in the child's general health, inappropriate educational placements, classroom rivalries, incompetent teaching, or mixed educational messages from the home and school. For example, it would be reasonable for a visually impaired child to act out in the classroom if the mathematics teacher spent 30 minutes a day having students solve problems written on the blackboard or for a preschooler to sit docilely in a language group without answering questions simply because she was not aware that she was being addressed. Both situations could arise from a teacher's lack of knowledge of the unique needs of visually impaired children; yet such children could be labeled as acting out or withdrawn. The files on such children could easily contain references to the child's inadequate adjustment or different behavior at home or the parents' need for training in behavioral management or help in accepting the child's disability.

Professionals who work with blind and visually impaired students and their families have the responsibility to approach the parent-professional relationship with the assumption that parents know their children best and that they care about their children's education. They also have the responsibility to be fair, to be active listeners, and to recognize their prejudices and inadequacies. The Division for the Visually Handicapped of the Council for Exceptional Children adopted a position paper (Hart & Ferrell, 1984) that suggests guidelines for parents and professionals to facilitate an environment that is conducive to the growth and learning of visually impaired children. The paper states that true parent-professional partnerships are based on respect, administration, and reasonable expectations for each other's roles. Such behavior ensures that

- Parents will be informed of their due process rights in language that is free of both educational and legal jargon, written at their educational level, and presented in an understandable auditory or visual format.

- Parents will be informed of the variety of services, techniques, and equipment that could be useful to their visually impaired child, instead of being informed of only those services which are currently available.

- Professionals will not discuss students' and families' affairs unless it is appropriate to the educational process, and then only in a professional context, and parents will treat professionals in the same manner.

- Permission forms will be specific, whether they refer to sharing medical records, transportation, participation in a research study, or photography; will not require blanket authorization by parents; and will offer parents the opportunity to limit or deny permission altogether (Hart & Ferrell, 1984).

Parents should no more place the professional on a pedestal than teachers should demand or expect perfection from the parents.

Federal and state requirements for parental involvement in the education of their children with disabilities imply that professionals should facilitate parents' movement through a continuum of activities—from passive and token attendance at IEP meetings, to active membership on advisory committees and boards of education, to the initiation of programs (Mori, 1983). Participants in professional meetings at which parents of visually impaired children have made presentations frequently comment that these parents were exceptions—that such active, involved, articulate parents were not found in most school districts. In reality, these "exceptional" parents are probably no different from other parents years ago. However, they probably have become dissatisfied with the educational programs provided to their children, and, it is hoped, have been encouraged, and supported by professionals to play gradually more important roles in these programs. There are no exceptional parents. But parents who are given the opportunity to become leaders and who work alongside professionals who have allowed them to realize their potential can and do become leading advocates for their children.

APPENDIX 1.

Principles of treatment of disabled infants

Discrimination of any type against any individual with a disability or disabilities, regardless of the nature or severity of the disability, is morally and legally indefensible. Throughout their lives, all disabled individuals have the same rights as other citizens, including access to such major societal activites as health care, education, and employment. These rights for all disabled persons must be recognized at birth.

Need for information

There is a need for professional education and dissemination of updated information that will improve decision making about disabled individuals, especially newborn infants. To this end, it is imperative to educate all persons involved in the decision-making process. Parents should be given information on available resources to assist in the care of their disabled infants. Society should be informed about the value and worth of disabled persons. Professional organizations, advocacy groups, the government, and individual caregivers should educate and inform the general public on the care, need, value, and worth of disabled infants.

Medical care

When medical care is clearly beneficial, it should always be provided. When appropriate medical care is not available, arrangements should be made to transfer the infant to an appropriate medical facility. Such considerations as an individual's anticipated or actual limited potential and the present or future lack of available community resources are irrelevant and must not determine decisions about medical care. The individual's medical condition should be the sole focus of the decision. These are strict standards.

It is ethically and legally justified to withhold medical or surgical procedures that are clearly futile and will only prolong the act of dying. However, supportive care should be provided, including sustenance as medically indicated and relief from pain and suffering. The needs of the dying person should be respected. The family also should be supported in its grieving.

When it is uncertain whether medical treatment will be beneficial, a person's disability must not be the basis for a decision to withhold treatment. At all times during the process when decisions are being made about the benefit or futility of medical treatment, the person should be cared for in the medically most appropriate ways. When doubt exists at any time about whether to treat, the presumption always should be in favor of treatment.

Governmental and community support

Once a decision to treat an infant has been made, governmental and private agencies must be prepared to allocate adequate resources for the services that are needed by the child and family for as long as they are needed. Services should be individualized, community based, and coordinated.

The federal government has an historical and legitimate role in protecting the rights of its citizens. Among these rights is the enforcement of all applicable federal statutes established to prevent and remedy discrimination against individuals with disabilities, including those afforded by Section 504 of the Rehabilitation Act. States also have legitimate roles in protecting the rights of their citizens and an obligation to enforce all applicable state laws.

References

Division of Educational Services, Special Education Programs (1984). *Sixth annual report to Congress on the implementation of Public Law 94-142: The Education for All Handicapped Children Act.* Washington, DC: U.S. Department of Education.

Ducanis, A.J., & Golin, A.K. (1979). *The interdisciplinary health care team.* Germantown, MD: Aspen Systems Corp.

Duff, R.S., & Campbell, A.G.M. (1973). Moral and ethical dilemmas in the special care nursery. *New England Journal of Medicine, 289,* 890-894.

Goldstein, S., Strickland, B., Turnbull, A.P., & Curry, L. (1980). Observational analysis of the IEP conference. *Exceptional children, 46,* 278-286.

Hart, V., & Ferrell, K.A. (1985). Parent/educator cooperative efforts in the education of the visually handicapped. In G.T. Scholl (Ed.), *Quality services for blind and visually handicapped learners: Statements of position.* Reston, VA: Council for Exceptional Children.

Heller, H.W. (Guest Ed.) (1983). Special education and professional standards. *Exceptional children, 50* (3), 2-32.

Kirchner, C. (1983). Special education for visually handicapped children: A critique of data on numbers served and costs [Statistical Brief #23]. *Journal of Visual Impairment & Blindness, 77,* 219-223.

Lynch, E. (1981). *Barriers to full participation of lower socioeconomic status parents of special education students in school activities.* San Diego, CA: San Diego State University.

Lyon, J. (1985). *Playing god in the nursery.* New York: W.W. Norton & Co.

Mori, A.A. (1973). *Families of children with special needs.* Rockville, MD: Aspen Systems Corp.

National Commission on Excellence in Education (1983). *A nation at risk: The imperative for educational reform. A report to the nation and the Secretary of Education, United States Department of Education.* Washington, DC: U.S. Department of Education.

Packer, J., & Kirchner, C. (1985). State-level counts on blind and visually handicapped preschool and school-aged children [Statistical Brief #31]. *Journal of Visual Impairment & Blindness, 79* (7), 357-361.

Parent involvement under 94-142. *Insight,* January 23, 1980.

Roit, M.L., & Pfohl, W. (1984). The readability of Public Law 94-142 parent materials: Are parents truly informed? *Exceptional Children, 50,* 496-505.

U.S. Department of Education (February, 1984). Application for grants under training personnel for the education of the handicapped (CFDA No. 84:029). Author.

Welsh, R.L., & Blasch, B.B. (Eds.) (1980). *Foundations of orientation and mobility.* New York: American Foundation for the Blind.

Legal requirements

This appendix outlines selected legal requirements that relate to programs serving blind and visually impaired students. Its purpose is to allow readers to review legal provisions established on the federal and state levels. Throughout this appendix, key federal regulations promulgated pursuant to the Education of All Handicapped Children Act (P.L. 94-142) and its amendments are followed by related state provisions. The state provisions shown were derived from the California Education Code and California Code of Regulations, and key sections are presented as an example of a state's legal requirements. The legal requirements outlined were current as of December 1988.

In general, federal laws and regulations are broader and less specific than those of individual states. Every state and commonwealth passes its own laws and regulations consistent with federal mandates as outlined in the state's annual program plan, which must be approved by the U.S. Department of Education in order for the state to receive P.L. 94-142 funds. Readers are urged to obtain copies of the laws and regulations in their states that deal with special education as well as federal laws and regulations. Copies of such legal requirements can usually be obtained from special education administrators and teachers, state vision consultants, members of Congress, state legislators, and many local libraries, particularly law libraries. Readers who wish to obtain copies of complete legal requirements can obtain them from their state's Department of Education. (See Appendix C.)

ELIGIBILITY CRITERIA FOR VISUALLY IMPAIRED STUDENTS

Code of Federal Regulations (34 CFR), sec. 300.5 (b)
(11) "Visually handicapped" means a visual impairment which, even with correction, adversely affects a child's educational performance. The term includes both partially seeing and blind children.

California Code of Regulations, Title 5, sec. 3030
(d) A pupil has a visual impairment which, even with

Federal provisions compiled by B. Joseph Ballard, Associate Director for Governmental Relations, Council for Exceptional Children.

correction, adversely affects a pupil's educational performance.

LOW-INCIDENCE DISABILITIES DEFINITIONS

Code of Federal Regulations (34 CFR), sec. 300.5
[Eligible handicapping conditions are defined, including "low-incidence" populations, i.e., "Deaf," "Hard of Hearing," "Orthopedically Handicapped," "Deaf-Blind," and "Visually Handicapped."]

California Education Code, sec. 56000.5
The Legislature finds and declares that:
(a) Pupils with low-incidence disabilities, as a group, make up less than 1 percent of the total statewide enrollment for kindergarten through grade 12.
(b) Pupils with low-incidence disabilities require highly specialized services, equipment, and materials.

sec. 56026.5
"Low-incidence disability" means a severe handicapping condition with an expected incidence rate of less than 1 percent of the total statewide enrollment in kindergarten through grade 12. For purposes of this definition, severe handicapping conditions are hearing impairments, vision impairments, and severe orthopedic impairments, or any combination thereof.

QUALIFIED STAFF/CREDENTIALING

Code of Federal Regulations (34 CFR), sec. 300.12
As used in this part, the term "qualified" means that a person has met State educational agency approved or recognized certification, licensing, registration, or other comparable requirements which apply to the area in which he or she is providing special education or related services.

California Education Code, sec. 56001
It is the intent of the Legislature that special education programs provide all of the following:
. . . (n) Appropriate qualified staff are employed, consistent with credentialing requirements, to fulfill the responsibilities of the local plan and that positive efforts to employ qualified handicapped individuals are made.

sec. 44265.5

(a) Pupils who are visually handicapped shall be taught by teachers who are credentialed pursuant to subdivision (e) of Section 44265. [This section refers to the Specialist in Special Education Credential for teachers of the blind and partially seeing.]

GUIDELINES/TECHNICAL ASSISTANCE/MONITORING

Code of Federal Regulations (34 CFR), sec. 300.384

(a) Each annual program plan must include a description of the State's procedures for acquiring, reviewing, and disseminating to general and special educational instructional and support personnel, administrators of programs for handicapped children, and other interested agencies and organizations (including parent, handicapped, and other advocacy organizations) significant information and promising practices derived from educational research, demonstration, and other projects.

(b) Dissemination includes:

(1) Making those personnel, administrators, agencies, and organizations aware of the information and practices;

(2) Training designed to enable the establishment of innovative programs and practices targeted on identified local needs; and

(3) Use of instructional materials and other media for personnel development and instructional programming.

sec. 300.385

(a) Each annual program must provide for a statewide system designed to adopt, where appropriate, promising educational practices and materials proven effective through research and demonstration.

(b) Each annual program plan must provide for thorough reassessment of educational practices used in the State.

(c) Each annual program plan must provide for the identification of State, local, and regional resources (human and material) which will assist in meeting the State's personnel preparation needs.

sec. 300.387

Each annual program plan must include a description of technical assistance that the State educational agency gives to local educational agencies in their implementation of the State's comprehensive system of personnel development.

sec. 300.402

In implementing Reg. 300.401, the State educational agency shall:

(a) Monitor compliance through procedures such as written reports, on-site visits, and parent questionnaires;

(b) Disseminate copies of applicable standards to each private school and facility to which a public agency has referred or placed a handicapped child; and

(c) Provide an opportunity for those private schools and facilities to participate in the development and revision of State standards which apply to them.

California Education Code, sec. 56136

The superintendent shall develop guidelines for each low-incidence disability area and provide technical assistance to parents, teachers, and administrators regarding the implementation of the guidelines. The guidelines shall clarify the identification, assessment, planning of, and the provision of, specialized services to pupils with low-incidence disabilities. The superintendent shall consider the guidelines when monitoring programs serving pupils with low-incidence disabilities pursuant to Section 56825. The adopted guildelines shall be promulgated for the purpose of establishing recommended guidelines and shall not operate to impose minimum state requirements.

DIRECTORIES OF PUBLIC AND PRIVATE AGENCIES

Code of Federal Regulations

[This subject is not discussed explicitly in the P.L. 94-142 regulations. Part H of P.L. 99-457 contains comparable material, however. See Appendix H for a discussion of P.L. 99-457.]

California Education Code, sec. 56137

The superintendent [State Superintendent of Public Instruction] shall develop, update every other year, and disseminate directories of public and private agencies providing services to pupils with low-incidence disabilities. The directories shall be made available as reference directories to parents, teachers, and administrators. The directories shall include, but need not be limited to, the following information:

(a) A description of each agency providing services and program options within each disability area.

(b) The specialized services and program options provided, including infant and preschool programs.

(c) The number of credentialed and certificated staff providing specialized services.

(d) The names, addresses, and telephone numbers of agency administrators or other individuals responsible for the programs.

COMPLIANCE ASSURANCES/ DESCRIPTION OF SERVICES

Code of Federal Regulations (34 CFR), sec. 300.180

In order to receive payments under Part B of the Act for any fiscal year a local educational agency must submit an application to the State educational agency.

sec. 300.222

Each application must:

(a) Include a goal of providing full educational opportunity to all handicapped children, aged birth through 21, and

(b) Include a detailed timetable for accomplishing the goal.

sec. 300.223

Each application must provide a description of the kind and number of facilities, personnel, and services necessary to meet the goal in Reg. 300.222.

[Code of Federal Regulations (34 CFR), sec. 300.182 through 300.221 and 300.224, describes additional requirements of local educational agencies.]

California Education Code, sec. 56200

Each local plan submitted to the superintendent [State Superintendent of Public Instruction] under this part shall contain all the following:

(a) Compliance assurances, including general compliance with Public Law 94-142, Section 504 of Public Law 93-112, and the provisions of this part.

(b) Description of services to be provided by each district and county office. Such description shall demonstrate that all individuals with exceptional needs shall have access to services and instruction appropriate to meet their needs as specified in their individualized education programs.

LOCAL PLAN AGREEMENTS

Code of Federal Regulations (34 CFR), sec. 300.220

Each application must include procedures which insure that all children residing within the jurisdiction of the local educational agency who are handicapped, regardless of the severity of their handicap, and who are in need of special education and related services are identified, located, and evaluated, including a practical method of determining which children are currently receiving needed special education and related services and which children are not currently receiving needed special education and related services.

Comment. The local educational agency is responsible for insuring that all handicapped children within its jurisdiction are identified, located and evaluated, including children in all public and private agencies and institutions within that jurisdiction. Collection and use of data are subject to the confidentiality requirements in Regs. 300.560-300.576 of Subpart E.

sec. 300.501

Each State educational agency shall insure that each public agency establishes and implements procedural safeguards which meet the requirements of Regs. 300.500-300.514.

[Code of Federal Regulations (34 CFR), sec. 300.131, 300.327, describes additional requirements related to procedural safeguards.]

California Education Code, sec. 56220

In addition to the provisions required to be included in the local plan pursuant to Section 56200, each special education services region that submits a local plan pursuant to subdivision (b) of Section 56170 and each county office that submits a local plan pursuant to subdivision (c) of Section 56170 shall develop written agreements to be entered into by entities participating in the plan. Such agreements need not be submitted to the superintendent. These agreements shall include, but not be limited to, the following:

(a) A coordinated identification, referral, and placement system pursuant to Chapter 4 (commencing with Section 56300).

(b) Procedural safeguards pursuant to Chapter 5 (commencing with Section 56500).

(c) Regionalized services to local programs, including, but not limited to, all the following:

(1) Program specialist service pursuant to Section 56368.

(2) Personnel development, including training for staff, parents, and members of the community advisory committee pursuant to Article 3 (commencing with Section 56240).

(3) Evaluation pursuant to Chapter 6 (commencing with Section 56600).

(4) Data collection and development of management information systems.

(5) Curriculum development.

(6) Provision for ongoing review of programs conducted, and procedures utilized, under the local plan, and a mechanism for correcting any identified problem.

(d) A description of the process for coordinating services

with other local public agencies which are funded to serve individuals with exceptional needs.

(e) A description of the process for coordinating and providing services to individuals with exceptional needs placed in public hospitals, proprietary hospitals, and possibly, other residential medical facilities pursuant to Article 5.5 (commencing with Section 56167) of Chapter 2.

(f) A description of the process for coordinating and providing services to individuals with exceptional needs placed in licensed children's institutions and foster family homes pursuant to Article 5 (commencing with Section 56155) of Chapter 2.

(g) This section shall become operative July 1, 1982.

TRANSPORTATION

Code of Federal Regulations (34 CFR), sec. 300.13b
(13) "Transportation" includes:
(i) Travel to and from school and between schools,
(ii) Travel in and around school buildings, and
(iii) Specialized equipment (such as special or adapted buses, lifts, and ramps), if required to provide special transportation for handicapped children.

California Education Code, sec. 56221
(a) Each entity providing special education under this part shall adopt policies for the programs and services it operates, consistent with agreements adopted pursuant to subdivision (b) or (c) of Section 56170, or Section 56220. The policies need not be submitted to the superintendent.
(b) Such policies shall include, but not be limited to, all of the following:
...(5) Transportation, where appropriate, which describes how special education transportation is coordinated with regular home-to-school transportation. The policy shall set forth criteria for meeting the transportation needs of special education pupils.

PERSONNEL/STAFF DEVELOPMENT

Code of Federal Regulations (34 CFR), sec. 300.380
Each annual program plan must include a description of programs and procedures for the development and implementation of a comprehensive system of personnel development which includes:
(a) The inservice training of general and special educational instructional, related services, and support personnel.

sec. 300.382
(a) As used in this section, "inservice training" means

any training other than that received by an individual in a full time program which leads to a degree.
(b) Each annual program plan must provide that the State educational agency:
(1) Conducts an annual needs assessment to determine if a sufficient number of qualified personnel are available in the State; and
(2) Initiates inservice personnel development programs based on the assessed needs of Statewide significance related to the implementation of the Act....

sec. 300.383
Each annual program plan must:
(a) Include a personnel development plan which provides a structure for personnel planning and focuses on preservice and in-service education needs;
(b) Describe the results of the needs assessment under Reg. 300.382 (b)(1) with respect to identifying needed areas of training, and assigning priorities to those areas; and
(c) Identify the target populations for personnel development, including general education and special education instructional and administrative personnel, support personnel, and other personnel (such as paraprofessionals, parents, surrogate parents, and volunteers).

[Code of Federal Regulations (34 CFR), sec. 300.38, sec. 300.384 through 300.387, and sec. 300.224, contains additional requirements related to personnel development.]

California Education Code, sec. 56240
Staff development programs shall be provided for regular and special education teachers, administrators, certificated and classified employees, volunteers, community advisory committee members and, as appropriate, members of the district and county governing boards. Such programs shall be coordinated with other staff development programs in the district, special education services region, or county office, including school level staff development programs authorized by state and federal law.

IDENTIFICATION AND REFERRAL

Code of Federal Regulations (34 CFR), sec. 300.128
(a) General requirement. Each annual program plan must include in detail the policies and procedures which the State will undertake or has undertaken to insure that:
(1) All children who are handicapped, regardless of the severity of their handicap, and who are in need of special education and related services are identified, located, and evaluated; and

(2) A practical method is developed and implemented to determine which children are currently receiving needed special education and related services and which children are not currently receiving needed special education and related services. . . .

(b) Information. Each annual program plan must:

(1) Designate the State agency (if other than the State educational agency) responsible for coordinating the planning and implementation of the policies and procedures under paragraph (a) of this section.

(2) Name each agency that participates in the planning and implementation and describe the nature and extent of its participation;

(3) Describe the extent to which:

(i) The activities described in paragraph (a) of this section have been achieved under the current annual program plan, and

(ii) The resources named for these activities in that plan have been used;

(4) Describe each type of activity to be carried out during the next school year, including the role of the agency named under paragraph (b)(1) of this section, timelines for completing those activities, resources that will be used, and expected outcomes;

(5) Describe how the policies and procedures under paragraph (a) of this section will be monitored to insure that the State educational agency obtains:

(i) The number of handicapped children within each disability category that have been identified, located, and evaluated, and

(ii) Information adequate to evaluate the effectiveness of those policies and procedures; and

(6) Describe the method the State uses to determine which children are currently receiving special education and related services and which children are not receiving special and related services.

Comment. The State is responsible for insuring that all handicapped children are identified, located, and evaluated, including children in all public and private agencies and institutions in the State. Collection and use of data are subject to the confidentiality requirements in Regs. 300.560-300.576 of Subpart E.

California Education Code, sec. 56300

Each district, special education services region, or county office shall actively and systematically seek out all individuals with exceptional needs, ages 0 through 21 years, including children not enrolled in public school programs, who reside in the district or are under the jurisdiction of a special education services region or a county office.

sec. 56301

Each district, special education services region, or county office shall establish written policies and procedures for a continuous child-find system which addresses the relationships among identification, screening, referral, assessment, planning, implementation, review, and the triennial assessment. Such policies and procedures shall include, but need not be limited to, written notification of all parents of their rights under this chapter, and the procedure for initiating a referral for assessment to identify individuals with exceptional needs.

sec. 56302

Each district, special education services region, or county office shall provide for the identification and assessment of an individual's exceptional needs, and the planning of an instructional program to best meet the assessed needs. Identification procedures shall include systematic methods of utilizing referrals of pupils from teachers, parents, agencies, appropriate professional persons, and from other members of the public. Identification procedures shall be coordinated with school site procedures for referral of pupils with needs that cannot be met with modification of the regular instructional program.

sec. 56303

A pupil shall be referred for special educational instruction and services only after the resources of the regular education program have been considered and, where appropriate, utilized.

ASSESSMENT/LOW VISION ASSESSMENT (EVALUATION)

Code of Federal Regulations (34 CFR), sec. 300.532

State and local educational agencies shall insure, at a minimum, that:

(a) Tests and other evaluation materials:

(1) Are provided and administered in the child's native language or other mode of communication, unless it is clearly not feasible to do so;

(2) Have been validated for the specific purpose for which they are used; and

(3) Are administered by trained personnel in conformance with the instructions provided by their producers;

(b) Tests and other evaluative materials include those tailored to assess specific areas of educational need and not merely those which are designed to provide a single general intelligence quotient;

(c) Tests are selected and administered so as best to ensure that when a test is administered to a child with impaired sensory, manual, or speaking skills, the test results accurately reflect the child's aptitude or achievement level or whatever other factors the test purports to measure, rather than reflecting the child's impaired sensory, manual, or speaking skills (except where those skills are the factors which the test purports to measure);

(d) No single procedure is used as the sole criterion for determining an appropriate educational program for a child; and

(e) The evaluation is made by a multidisciplinary team or group of persons, including at least one teacher or other specialist with knowledge in the area of suspected disability.

(f) The child is assessed in all areas related to the suspected disability, including, where appropriate, health, vision, hearing, social and emotional status, general intelligence, academic performance, communicative status, and motor abilities.

sec. 300.533

(a) In interpreting evaluation data and in making placement decisions, each public agency shall:

(1) Draw upon information from a variety of sources, including aptitude and achievement tests, teacher recommendations, physical condition, social or cultural background, and adaptive behavior;

(2) Insure that information obtained from all of these sources is documented and carefully considered;

(3) Insure that the placement decision is made by a group of persons, including persons knowledgeable about the child, the meaning of the evaluation data, and the placement options; and

(4) Insure that the placement decision is made in conformity with the least restrictive environment rules in Regs. 300.550-300.554.

(b) If a determination is made that a child is handicapped and needs special education and related services, an individualized education program must be developed for the child in accordance with Regs. 400.340-300.349 of Subpart C.

California Education Code, sec. 56320

(f) The pupil is assessed in all areas related to the suspected disability, including, where appropriate, health and development, vision, including low vision, hearing, motor abilities, language function, general ability, academic performance, self-help, orientation and mobility skills, career and vocational abilities and inter-

ests, and social and emotional status. A developmental history is obtained, when appropriate. For pupils with residual vision, a low vision assessment shall be provided in accordance with guidelines established pursuant to Section 56136.

(g) The assessment of a pupil, including the assessment of a pupil with a suspected low-incidence disability, shall be conducted by persons knowledgeable of that disability. Special attention shall be given to the unique educational needs, including, but not limited to, skills and the need for specialized services, materials, and equipment consistent with guidelines established pursuant to Section 56136.

sec. 56327

The personnel who assess the pupil shall prepare a written report, or reports, as appropriate, of the results of each assessment. The report shall include, but not be limited to, all the following:

. . . (h) The need for specialized services, materials, and equipment for pupils with low-incidence disabilities consistent with guidelines established pursuant to Section 56136.

VISUAL PERCEPTUAL/VISUAL MOTOR DYSFUNCTION/SPECIFIC LEARNING DISABILITY

Code of Federal Regulations (34 CFR), sec. 300.5 (B)

(9) "Specific learning disability" means a disorder in one or more of the basic psychological processes involved in understanding or in using language, spoken or written, which may manifest itself in an imperfect ability to listen, think, speak, read, write, spell, or to do mathematical calculations. The term includes such conditions as perceptual handicaps, brain injury, minimal brain dysfunction, dyslexia, and developmental aphasia. The term does not include children who have learning problems which are primarily the result of visual, hearing, or motor handicaps, of mental retardation, of emotional disturbance, or of environmental, cultural, or economic disadvantage.

California Education Code, sec. 56338

As used in Section 56337, "specific learning disability" includes, but is not limited to, disability within the function of vision which results in visual perceptual or visual motor dysfunction.

INDIVIDUALIZED EDUCATION PROGRAM

Code of Federal Regulations

[Code of Federal Regulations does not contain anything

as specific as the California requirement that follows; however, (34 CFR) sec. 300.346(c) requires the following to be included in the individualized education program:

(c) A statement of the specific special education and related services to be provided to the child, and the extent to which the child will be able to participate in regular educational programs....

[Code of Federal Regulations (34 CFR), sec. 300.340 through 300.452 and 300.554, describes additional requirements related to individualized education programs.]

California Education Code, sec. 56345

(b) When appropriate, the individualized education program shall also include, but not be limited to,...

(7) For pupils with low-incidence disabilities, specialized services, materials, and equipment, consistent with guidelines established pursuant to Section 56136.

CONTINUUM OF PROGRAM OPTIONS

Code of Federal Regulations (34 CFR), sec. 300.551

(a) Each public agency shall insure that a continuum of alternative placements is available to meet the needs of handicapped children for special education and related services.

(b) The continuum required under paragraph (a) of this section must:

(1) Include the alternative placements listed in the definition of special education under Reg. 300.13 of Subpart A (instruction in regular classes, special classes, special schools, home instruction, and instruction in hospitals and institutions, and

(2) Make provision for supplementary services (such as resource room or itinerant instruction) to be provided in conjunction with regular class placement.

California Education Code, sec. 56360

Each district, special education services region, or county office shall ensure that a continuum of program options is available to meet the needs of individuals with exceptional needs for special education and related services.

RELATED SERVICES/DESIGNATED INSTRUCTION AND SERVICES

Code of Federal Regulations (34 CFR), sec. 300.13

(a) As used in this part, the term "related services" means transportation and such developmental, corrective, and other supportive services as are required to assist a handicapped child to benefit from special educa-

tion, and includes speech pathology and audiology, psychological services, physical and occupational therapy, recreation, early identification and assessment of disabilities in children, counseling services, and medical services for diagnostic or evaluation purposes. The term also includes school health services, social work services in schools, and parent counseling and training....

California Education Code, sec. 56363

(a) Designated instruction and services as specified in the individualized education program shall be available when the instruction and services are necessary for the pupil to benefit educationally from his or her instructional program. The instruction and services shall be provided by the regular class teacher, the special class teacher, or the resource specialist if the teacher or specialist is competent to provide such instruction and services and if the provision of such instruction and services by the teacher or specialist is feasible. If not, the appropriate designated instruction and services specialist shall provide such instruction and services. Designated instruction and services shall meet standards adopted by the board.

(b) These services may include, but are not limited to, the following:

(1) Language and speech development and remediation.
(2) Audiological services.
(3) Orientation and mobility instruction.
(4) Instruction in the home or hospital.
(5) Adapted physical education.
(6) Physical and occupational therapy.
(7) Vision services.
(8) Specialized driver training instruction.
(9) Counseling and guidance.
(10) Psychological services other than assessment and development of the individualized education program.
(11) Parent counseling and training.
(12) Health and nursing services.
(13) Social worker services.
(14) Specially designed vocational education and career development.
(15) Recreation services.
(16) Specialized services for low-incidence disabilities, such as readers, transcribers, and vision and hearing services.

INTEGRATED SPECIAL CLASSES/INSTRUCTION

Code of Federal Regulations (34 CFR), sec. 300.550

(a) Each State educational agency shall insure that each

public agency establishes and implements procedures which meet the requirements of Regs. 300.550-300.556.
(b) Each public agency shall insure:
(1) That to the maximum extent appropriate, handicapped children, including children in public or private institutions or other care facilities, are educated with children who are not handicapped....

[See also sec. 300.551 under "Continuum of Program Options."]

California Education Code, sec. 56364.1
Notwithstanding the provisions of Section 56364 [which describes special classes], pupils with low-incidence disabilities may receive all or a portion of their instruction in the regular classroom and may also be enrolled in special classes taught by appropriately credentialed teachers who serve these pupils at one or more school sites. The instruction shall be provided in a manner which is consistent with the guidelines adopted pursuant to Section 56136 and in accordance with the individualized education program.

FUNDING SPECIALIZED BOOKS, MATERIALS, AND EQUIPMENT

Code of Federal Regulations
[The code does not include any specific funding requirements in this area.]

California Education Code, sec. 56739
(a) When allocating funds received for special education pursuant to this article, it is the intent of the Legislature that, to the extent funding is available, school districts and county offices shall give first priority to expenditures to provide specialized books, materials, and equipment which are necessary and appropriate for the individualized education programs of pupils with low-incidence disabilities, up to a maximum of five hundred dollars ($500) per pupil with low-incidence disability. Nothing in this subdivision shall be construed to prohibit pooling the prioritized funds to purchase equipment to be shared by several pupils.
(b) Equipment purchased pursuant to this section shall include, but not necessarily be limited to, nonprescriptive equipment, sensory aids, and other equipment and materials as appropriate.

sec. 56771
(a) Commencing with the 1985-86 fiscal year, and for each fiscal year thereafter, funds to support specialized books, materials, and equipment as required under the individualized education program for each pupil with low-incidence disabilities, as defined in Section 56026.5, shall be determined by dividing the total number of pupils with low-incidence disabilities in the state, as reported on December 1 of the prior fiscal year, into the annual appropriation provided for this purpose in the Budget Act.
(b) The per-pupil entitlement determined pursuant to subdivision (a) shall be multiplied by the number of pupils with low-incidence disabilities in each special education local plan area to determine the total funds available for each local plan.
(c) The superintendent [State Superintendent of Public Instruction] shall apportion the amount determined pursuant to subdivision (b) to the responsible local agency in the special education local plan area for purposes of purchasing and coordinating the use of specialized books, materials, and equipment.
(d) As a condition of receiving these funds, the responsible local agency shall ensure that the appropriate books, materials, and equipment are purchased, that the use of the equipment is coordinated as necessary, and that the books, materials, and equipment are reassigned to local educational agencies within the special education local plan area once the agency that originally received the books, materials, and equipment no longer needs them.
(e) It is the intent of the Legislature that special education local plan areas share unused specialized books, materials, and equipment with neighboring special education local plan areas.

sec. 56822
Sound recordings, large type, and braille books purchased, instructional materials transcribed from regular print into special media, and special supplies and equipment purchased for individuals with exceptional needs for which state or federal funds were allowed are property of the state and shall be available for use by individuals with exceptional needs throughout the state as the board shall provide.

Provisions of P.L. 99-457

The passage of the Amendments to the Education for All Handicapped Children Act (P.L. 99-457) on October 30, 1986 significantly changed the availability of early intervention and preschool services to children with special needs. The amendments expand and improve various discretionary programs that are part of services relating to the Education for All Handicapped Children Act (P.L. 94-142) and include two new major provisions that have implications for the delivery of services to children with visual impairments:

1. By the 1990-91 school year, the provision of educational services will be mandated for all children with disabilities who are age 3 or older. This requirement represents a downward extension of eligibility for services from age 6. If Congress fails to appropriate the necessary funds, states will be granted an additional year to implement services fully.

2. The law offers a strong incentive for each state to provide services to children from birth, according to regulations and procedures outlined in the amendments, through the establishment of a new Early Intervention State Grant Program.

Services for children ages 3 through 5 years are to be provided under the same requirements, rights, and protections as those provided for children and young people ages 6 through 21 years according to P.L. 94-142, with a major exception. Children 3 through 5 do not have to be identified and counted as members of a specific categorical disability group according to criteria described in P.L. 94-142 to receive preschool services. All other programmatic components of P.L. 94-142 apply to services for children ages 3 to 5 years, including, but not limited to (1) a free, appropriate education in the least restrictive environment, (2) nonbiased assessment by a multidisciplinary team, (3) development of an individualized education program (IEP) by a multidisciplinary team, (4) regular review of placement and program, (5) right to confidentiality and parental involvement during all phases of programming, and (6) guarantee of rights of due process.

Services for children from birth through 2 years are to be provided as appropriate to the child's and the family's needs. Children are eligible for early childhood services if they are identified as experiencing a developmental delay or as being at risk of a substantial developmental delay according to state-established criteria, or if they have a diagnosed physical or mental condition that has a high probability of resulting in a developmental delay. Each child with an impairment or at risk for developmental delay is eligible to undergo early identification, screening, and assessment by a multidisciplinary team. As described in P.L. 99-457, services are to be delivered by qualified personnel at no cost, except in cases where federal or state law provides for a system of payments by families. Services must meet state standards and include as appropriate but are not limited to the following:

- family training, counseling, and home visits
- special instruction
- speech pathology and audiology
- occupational therapy
- physical therapy
- psychological services
- case management
- medical services for diagnosis for evaluation only
- early identification, screening, and assessment
- health services necessary to assist the child to benefit from other early intervention services.

Each child and family receive services appropriate to meet their needs as specified in a written Individual Family Service Plan (IFSP) developed by the family and the multidisciplinary team. The IFSP must be reviewed every six months and evaluated at least annually. Specific components of the IFSP include

- a statement of the child's present level of development
- a statement of the family's strengths and needs as they relate to assisting the child
- a statement of anticipated major outcomes to be achieved and how progress is to be measured
- identification of the specific early intervention services to be delivered, including the frequency, intensity, and method of delivery

Compiled by Alana M. Zambone, National Consultant in Multiple Disabilities and Early Childhood, American Foundation for the Blind.

SOURCE: Much of the information in this appendix was derived from *Facts: Public Law 99-457, Amendments to the Education of the Handicapped Act* (Arlington, TX: Association for Retarded Citizens, October 1986).

- identification of the case manager for implementation of the plan and coordination with other agencies
- transitional steps to special education services offered under P.L. 94-142.

Children and parents are protected under procedural safeguards that address (1) the timely resolution of administrative complaints and the right to appeal to a federal or state court, (2) the confidentiality of personal, identifiable information, (3) the opportunity to examine records, (4) the provision of services pending resolution of the complaint, and (5) procedures to protect the child if parents or guardians are not known or are unavailable, or if the child is a ward of the state.

Each state's governor may designate a single lead agency to carry out the program for children from birth through 2 years of age. The lead agency is responsible for the general administration, supervision, and monitoring of program and activities, coordination of resources, interagency agreements, and resolution of disputes. (The lead agency in each state and territory is identified in Table 1.) The governor is also required to appoint a

Table 1. Lead Agencies for P.L. 99-457 Programs

State	Lead agency
Alabama	Education
Alaska	Health and Social Services
American Samoa	Health
Arizona	Economic Security—Developmental Disabilities
Arkansas	Human Services
California	Developmental Services
Colorado	Education
Connecticut	Education
Delaware	Public Instruction
District of Columbia	Human Services
Florida	Education
Georgia	Human Resources
Guam	Education
Hawaii	Health (Crippled Services)
Idaho	Health and Welfare— Developmental Disabilities
Illinois	Education
Indiana	Mental Health
Iowa	Education
Kansas	Health and Environment

State	Lead agency
Kentucky	Cabinet for Human Resources
Louisiana	Education
Maine	Interdepartmental Committee
Mariana Islands	Education
Maryland	Office of Children and Youth
Massachusetts	Public Health
Michigan	Education
Minnesota	Education
Mississippi	Health
Missouri	Education
Montana	Developmental Disabilities
Nebraska	Education
Nevada	Human Resources
New Hampshire	Education
New Jersey	Education
New Mexico	Health and Environment
New York	Health
North Carolina	Human Resources
North Dakota	Human Services
Ohio	Health Department
Oklahoma	Education
Oregon	Mental Health Program for Developmental Disabilities
Pennsylvania	Public Welfare
Puerto Rico	Education
Rhode Island	Interagency Coordinating Council
South Carolina	Health and Environmental Control
South Dakota	Education and Cultural Affairs
Tennessee	Education
Texas	Interagency Council on Early Childhood Intervention
Utah	Health
Vermont	Education
Virginia	Mental Health/Mental Retardation
Virgin Islands	Health
Washington	Social and Health Services
West Virginia	Health
Wisconsin	Health and Social Services
Wyoming	Health and Human Services

SOURCE: The information shown in this table was provided by the National Association of State Directors of Special Education, Washington, DC, July 1987.

State Interagency Coordinating Council that may serve as the state's lead agency. The council consists of 15 members, including at least three parents of disabled children who are ages 3 through 6. The council's primary function is to assist the state's lead agency in preparing the early intervention grant application, identifying fiscal and other support, assigning financial responsibility to the appropriate agencies, and promoting interagency agreements.

As of July 1987, all 50 states, the District of Columbia, and the five trusts and territories agreed to participate in the new Early Intervention State Grant Fund. Thus, the provisions described are applicable for all states. Parents and other concerned parties who wish to obtain services can contact the lead agency in their state or territory or their state Department of Education.

Selected reading list

BOOKS, MONOGRAPHS, AND PAMPHLETS

American Foundation for the Blind Directory of Services for Blind and Visually Impaired Persons in the United States, 23rd Edition. (1988). New York: American Foundation for the Blind.
A resource directory of agencies and other organizations of and for blind and visually impaired persons. Services offered by the federal government are listed, along with those provided by state and voluntary agencies, schools, and national organizations.

Berdine, W.H., and Blackhurst, A.E. (1985). *An Introduction to Special Education* (2nd ed.). Boston: Little, Brown and Company.
A textbook and comprehensive survey of the field of special education. Fourteen chapters are divided into four parts: the first contains information critical to an understanding of all areas of special education; the second examines communication and sensorimotor disabilities; the third examines individual differences in learning and behavior; and the fourth discusses the development of career and vocational education programs for exceptional learners as well as the role of the family.

California Leadership Action Team for the Visually Impaired. (1985). *Statement of Educational Needs of Visually Impaired Students in California*. Unpublished monograph. Available through the American Foundation for the Blind, National Services in Education, Low Vision and Orientation & Mobility Department in New York and all AFB Regional Centers as well as the California State Department of Education. (See Appendixes A and C for addresses.)
A comprehensive 5-page statement that is appropriate for distribution to school administrators and related service providers unfamiliar with the unique learning needs of blind and visually impaired students. It identifies six barriers to learning and nine unique areas of study and briefly discusses the interplay of visual impairment with other impairments; teacher competencies; and a continuum of services and program options. This monograph was adopted by the California Low Incidence Disability Advisory Committee (LIDAC).

Career Choice for Blind and Visually Impaired Students: Career Planning and Placement Offices. (1985). New York: American Foundation for the Blind.
Information, tips, and ideas drawn from a national survey of college placement officers on the special needs—and the special skills—of blind and visually impaired students and how to reach and work with these students.

Davis, W.E. (1986). *Resource Guide to Special Education: Terms/Laws/Assessment Procedures/Organizations* (2nd ed.). Boston: Allyn and Bacon.

A valuable resource for special educators, regular classroom teachers, school administrators, community agency personnel, parents of students with special needs, students preparing for careers in special education and related fields, and a wide variety of other professionals who have an interest in the special education field. The five major sections deal with terminology employed in special education and related areas, selected acronyms and abbreviations used in special education and related fields, selected assessment procedures, federal legislation and litigation related to handicapped persons, and selected agencies and organizations concerned with exceptional persons.

Falvey, M.A. (1986). *Community Based Curriculum: Instructional Strategies for Students with Severe Handicaps*. Baltimore: Paul H. Brookes Publishing.
Strategies for developing and implementing appropriate educational programs for individuals with severe handicaps are provided for parents, educators, therapists, counselors, and other concerned individuals. Topics covered include assessment and instruction; community, domestic, recreation/leisure, vocational, motor, communication, and functional academic skills; and integration issues and strategies.

Ferrell, K. (1984). *Parenting Preschoolers: Suggestions for Raising Young Blind and Visually Impaired Children*. New York: American Foundation for the Blind.
Answers to the most frequent questions of parents who have just learned that their child has vision problems. Topics include what to expect if a child is blind or visually handicapped, when and if a cane will be needed, where to get help, and how to choose an early childhood program. Basic definitions, references, and agency lists are also provided.

Ferrell, K. (1985). *Reach Out and Teach: Materials for Parents of Visually Handicapped and Multihandicapped Young Children*. New York: American Foundation for the Blind.
Materials in this 2-volume set are intended to give parents the information they need (and have asked for) in raising their visually or multiply handicapped children; the suggestions were field-tested over two years. The *Parent Handbook* is a 7-chapter overview of early child development and activities and training techniques in all areas of motor and cognitive development and coincides with the *Reachbook*, in which parents can enter information and keep records of their child's progress. The *Slide/Tape Presentation* gives an introduction to the information in the *Parent Handbook*, and the *Teacher's Manual* helps teachers adapt the material for their own work.

Goldman, C.D. (1987). *Disability Rights Guide: Practical Solutions to Problems Affecting People With Disabilities*. Lincoln, NE: Media Publishing.

A guide for disabled and nondisabled people alike who are concerned with the problems of persons with physical or mental limitations. A conceptual framework and complementary practical solutions are provided to address issues relating to attitudinal barriers, employment, accessibility, housing, education, and transportation.

Harrell, L., and Akeson, N. (1987). *Preschool Vision Stimulation: It's More than a Flashlight! Developmental Perspectives for Visually and Multihandicapped Infants and Preschoolers*. New York: American Foundation for the Blind.
For both parents and professionals who work with visually impaired children, carefully researched procedures for preschool vision stimulation are described, along with the philosophical justification for these procedures and the implications of visual impairment for early development.

Heward, W. L., and Orlansky, M.D. (1988). *Exceptional Children: An Introductory Survey of Special Education* (3rd ed.). Columbus, OH: Merrill Publishing.
A highly popular introduction to special education textbooks that is used throughout the country. Nine chapters are presented by disability area and include definitions and information on prevalence, causes, education, treatment, and management as well as current issues and future trends. Other chapters provide basic information on special education, early intervention, legislation, parents and families, cultural diversity, and services for adults.

Jan, J.E., Freeman, R.D., and Scott, E.P. (1977). *Visual Impairment in Children and Adolescents*. New York: Grune & Stratton.
A comprehensive textbook covering definitions, causes, ocular disorders, prevention, evaluation and psychological testing, stereotyped behavior, counseling, and deaf-blindness.

Jose, R. (Ed.). (1983). *Understanding Low Vision*. New York: American Foundation for the Blind.
A 20-chapter overview of the state of the art and developing trends in the provision of care for persons with low vision. The book presents a framework for understanding the impact of low vision (or loss of vision) on functioning, learning, and psychosocial status and also examines professional services and future directions for the field. Experts from 21 areas contributed chapters, reports, and technical information.

Kirchner, C. (1988). *Data on Blindness and Visual Impairment in the U.S., 2nd Edition*. New York: American Foundation for the Blind.
An accessible source of information presenting data, analyses, and the social, educational, and employment characteristics of blind and visually impaired persons in the United States and reporting on the delivery of services to that population. This collection of 28 "Statistical Briefs" originally published in the *Journal of Visual Impairment & Blindness* offers concise, valuable, and timely demographic information particularly useful for policy planners and researchers.

Low Vision Questions and Answers: Definitions, Devices, Services. (1987). New York: American Foundation for the Blind.

Definitions and options for visually impaired people are discussed in a straightforward question-and-answer format that covers such topics as diagnosis, treatment, services, devices, and attitudes. Estimates show that 80 percent of the people classified as "legally blind" in the United States may actually belong in the low vision category.

Mangold, S.S. (Ed.). (1982). *A Teacher's Guide to the Special Educational Needs of Blind and Visually Handicapped Children*. New York: American Foundation for the Blind.
A multidisciplinary approach to the education of visually handicapped students, with each chapter focusing on a unique educational need. Teaching reading via braille, orientation to low vision needs, sexuality, nurturing high self-esteem, art experience, and aural reading are some of the areas covered.

Mendelsohn, S.B. (1987). *Financing Adaptive Technology: A Guide to Sources and Strategies for Blind and Visually Impaired Users*. New York: Smiling Interface.
Useful information on the vocational rehabilitation system, other programs of state blindness agencies, the Social Security Administration, credit systems, the tax code, the education system, and miscellaneous sources of financing such as veterans' insurance benefits, service clubs, civic organizations, and foundation grants. The final chapter discusses what agencies can do.

Olson, M.R. (1981). *Guidelines and Games for Teaching Efficient Braille Reading*. New York: American Foundation for the Blind.
Games and accompanying guidelines for teaching children to read braille efficiently. Based on research in rapid reading and precision teaching, the material presents unique methods for adapting a general reading program to the needs of braille readers.

Rogow, S.M. (1988). *Helping the Visually Impaired Child with Developmental Problems: Effective Practice in Home, School, and Community*. New York: Teachers College Press.
Nine comprehensive chapters focusing on visually impaired children who are developmentally delayed or have additional developmental handicaps. The first chapter presents the dynamic interactionist model of intervention and is the basis for the structure and methodology used throughout the book. The second chapter examines the nature of intervention in infancy and early childhood; the next two familiarize readers with visual impairments and concepts relating to learning capabilities. Others discuss the developmental consequences of impairments and various educational interventions, covering communication skills, play and social interaction, listening skills, prosthetic equipment, and technology.

Scholl, G.T. (1986). *Foundations of Education for Blind and Visually Handicapped Children and Youth: Theory and Practice*. New York: American Foundation for the Blind.
A unique resource detailing current options in the education of blind and visually impaired children, from preschool through high school. Major sections cover the history of education for visually impaired children; growth and development; educa-

tional theory; components of a high-quality educational program; low vision and visual efficiency; severe multiple handicaps; psychoeducational assessment; resources, media, and technology; social skills; curricular adaptations; and the transition to adulthood. Twenty-six specialists contributed material to 22 chapters.

Stein, H.A., Slatt, B.J., and Stein, R.M. (1987). *Ophthalmic Terminology: Speller and Vocabulary Builder* (2nd ed.). St. Louis: C.V. Mosby Company.
A handy reference manual designed for those unfamiliar with ophthalmic terminology. Containing 166 illustrations, the book covers the topics of basic science; refraction, spectacles, and contact lenses; disorders of the eye; surgery of the eye; and ophthalmic tests and devices and miscellaneous terms.

Swallow, R.M., and Huebner, K.M. (Eds.). (1987). *How to Thrive, Not Just Survive: A Guide to Developing Independent Life Skills for Visually Impaired Children and Youths*. New York: American Foundation for the Blind.
Guidelines and strategies for helping visually impaired children develop and apply skills necessary for independence in socialization, orientation and mobility, and leisure-time and recreational activities. Designed for parents, grandparents, babysitters, and others involved in the education of blind and visually impaired children and youths.

Warren, D.H. (1984). *Blindness and Early Childhood Development* (2nd ed.). New York: American Foundation for the Blind.
A comprehensive review of research and current knowledge about the effects of visual impairment on child development, encompassing motor and locomotor skills, perceptual abilities, language and cognitive processes, and social, emotional, and personality development. Also discusses areas in critical need of more research and the shortcomings of the available research literature.

Welsh, R., and Blasch, B.B. (Eds.). (1980). *Foundations of Orientation and Mobility*. New York: American Foundation for the Blind.
The basic textbook of theory and practice in a critical area relating to visual impairment and blindness. Twenty authors contributed chapters on a variety of topics, including environmental orientation and human mobility, audition, concept development, orientation aids, mobility devices, additional impairments, environmental modifications, and dog guides.

Yeadon, A. (1988). *The International Low Vision Directory*. Philadelphia: Institute for the Visually Impaired, Pennsylvania College of Optometry.
A directory that includes information on international organizations, national organizations, low vision clinics and rehabilitation services, low vision education programs, low vision resource specialists, low vision publications, manufacturers and producers, low vision research studies, and Veterans Administration resources and an advertising resource section. The introductions to the directory include an article on the challenges in the field of low vision care.

JOURNALS AND NEWSLETTERS

AER Report
Job Exchange Monthly
Re-view
Association for Education and Rehabilitation of the Blind and Visually Impaired
206 North Washington Street, Suite 320
Alexandria, VA 22314

AFB News
Journal of Visual Impairment & Blindness
American Foundation for the Blind
15 West 16th Street
New York, NY 10011

Awareness Newsletter
National Association for Parents of the Visually Impaired
P.O. Box 562
Camden, NY 13316

The Braille Monitor
Future Reflections
National Federation of the Blind
1800 Johnson Street
Baltimore, MD 21230

Exceptional Children
Council for Exceptional Children
1920 Association Drive
Reston, VA 22091

Exceptional Parent
P.O. Box 3000
Department EP
Denville, NJ 07834

Reflections Newsletter
American Council of the Blind Parents
c/o American Council of the Blind
1010 Vermont Avenue, N.W., Suite 1100
Washington, DC 20005

Ruralink Newsletter
Rural Special Education Quarterly
American Council on Rural Special Education
National Rural Development Institute
Western Washington University
Miller Hall 359
Bellingham, WA 98225

TASH Newsletter
The Journal of the Association for Persons with Severe Handicaps
Association for Persons with Severe Handicaps
7010 Roosevelt Way, N.E.
Seattle, WA 98115

Glossary

The terms included in this glossary relate to such areas as services, treatment, and medication for blind and visually impaired students and the nature of certain visual impairments.[1]

Accommodation. The adjustment of the eye to focus at different distances, accomplished through muscle action that changes the shape of the lens.

Adapted physical education. A diversified program of developmental activities, physical fitness, games, sports, and rhythmic movement suited to the needs, interests, capacities, and limitations of students who may not safely or successfully engage in unrestricted participation in the vigorous activities of a general physical education program.

Adaptive behavior. A reaction that promotes the social or biological welfare of an organism and leads to the adjustment of the organism to its environment.

Adventitious. Occurring after birth; not present at birth; (of blindness) occurring after visual memory is established.

Albinism. Congenital absence or deficiency of pigment in the iris, skin, or hair, usually associated with lowered visual acuity, nystagmus, and photophobia and often accompanied by large refractive errors.

Amblyopia. Diminished visual acuity, not correctable with conventional lenses and unrelated to structural or pathological ocular defects.

Aniridia. Congenital or acquired absence of the iris.

Anomaly. A marked deviation from the normal standard.

Anophthalmos (anophthalmia). Absence of a true eyeball.

Aphakia. Absence of the lens of the eye as a result of surgery, trauma, or a congenital condition.

Aqueous humor. Watery fluid that lies just behind the cornea and helps maintain the shape of the eye.

Astigmatism. Refractive error that prevents light rays from coming to a point or focus on the retina.

Aural. Pertaining to the ear; hearing.

Binocular vision. The ability to use both eyes simultaneously to focus on the same object and to fuse the two images into a single perception.

Blind. Unable to see; experiencing absence or severe reduction of vision. (See **Functionally blind; Legally blind.**)

Blind spot. A blank area in the visual field, corresponding to

the position of the optic nerve. In addition to occurring naturally, blind spots may occur as a result of damage to the retina and are referred to as scotomas.

Braille. A system of raised dots used to enable functionally blind persons to read by touch.

Braillewriter. A machine used to produced embossed braille symbols.

Cataract. A condition in which the lens of the eye partially or totally loses transparency, with consequent loss of visual acuity.

Central visual acuity. The ability of the macula to separate the details of images brought to a focus on it.

Choroid. Part of the eye that lies between the sclera and the inner retinal layer. Its function is to provide nutrients to the retina.

Choroiditis. Inflammation of the choroid.

Closed-circuit television (CCTV). A device in which printed material is electronically enlarged and appears on a television screen. All models allow the user to alter the degree of illumination and magnification; some allow the user to reverse the print and background colors.

Cognitive skills. Intellectual processing abilities.

Color deficiency. Partial or complete inability to discriminate the ordinarily differentiated colors.

Communication skills. The many ways of expressing thoughts through such media as speech, written words, body gestures, braille, and sign language.

Cones and rods. Two kinds of cells that form the photoreceptor layer of the retina and act as light-receiving media. Cones provide visual acuity and color discrimination; rods are sensitive to motion and vision at low degrees of illumination but not to color and are therefore important for night vision.

Congenital. Present at birth; (of blindness) occurring before visual memory is established.

Conjunctiva. Mucous membrane that forms the posterior layer of the eyelids and covers the front part of the eyeball.

Contact lenses. Lenses made to fit directly on the cornea. They are used to correct refractive errors such as hyperopia (farsightedness) and myopia (nearsightedness). They are also worn for cosmetic reasons. Contact lenses are sometimes used after cataract extraction to replace the clouded lens that is removed from the eye.

Cornea. Clear, transparent portion of the outer coat of the eyeball. The cornea is the major refracting medium of the eye.

Corneal scarring. A lack of transparency of the ordinarily clear corneal tissue.

Count fingers (CF). A method of reporting vision that is insufficient for the reading of the Snellen chart, in which the examiner records the number of inches at which the individual can differentiate and count upheld fingers.

---

[1]For definitions of ophthalmological and technical terms, the following books are examples of those that can be consulted: H.A. Stein, B.J. Slatt, and R.M. Stein, *Ophthalmic Terminology: Speller and Vocabulary Builder* (2d ed.; St. Louis, MO: C.V. Mosby Company, 1987) and D. Vaughn and T. Asbury, *General Ophthalmology* (11th ed.; Los Altos, CA: Lange Medical Publications, 1986).

Daily living skills. Skills that enable a blind or visually impaired person to perform routine activities necessary to live independently.

Dark adaptation. The ability of the retina and pupil to adjust to dim light.

Depth perception. The ability to perceive the solidity of objects and their relative position in space.

Diffused light. Light spread out and covering a large space or area.

Diopter. Unit of measurement of lens power.

Diplopia. The seeing of one object as two.

Direct lighting. Light with no shield. Direct lighting often creates glare.

Distance vision. The ability to see objects clearly from a distance.

Enucleation. Complete surgical removal of the eyeball.

Esotropia. A manifest turning inward of the eye.

Exotropia. A manifest turning outward of the eye.

Extraocular. Outside the eyeball.

Extraocular motility. The ability to move the eyes from one position to another.

Eye specialist. A licensed ophthalmologist or optometrist.

Farnsworth test. A measurement of color perception using a series of plastic chips of slightly differing hues.

Farsightedness. Hyperopia.

Federal quota program. Program funded by Congress and administered by the American Printing House for the Blind in Louisville, Kentucky, to supply educational materials to blind and visually impaired students. (See **Appendix B**.)

Fixation ability. The ability of the eyes to direct a person's gaze on an object and to hold the object steadily in view.

Focus. The point to which rays are converged after passing through a lens.

Foot candle. The unit commonly used to measure light intensity; the amount of light given off by a candle at a 1-foot distance.

Fovea. A pit or depression; a rodless area of the retina affording acute vision.

Free matter for the blind. Material mailed free to blind people under mailing privileges permitted by federal regulation.

Functionally blind. Using senses other than sight as the major channel for learning.

Functional vision. Vision usable enough for the performance of desired tasks.

Fusion. The power of coordinating the images received by the two eyes into a single mental image.

Glare. A quality of light that causes discomfort in the eye; it may result from a direct light source within the field of vision or from a reflection of a light source not in the field of vision.

Glaucoma. A disease of the eye marked by an increase in the intraocular pressure that may cause organic changes in the optic nerve and defects in the visual field.

Halberg clips. Lens holders that can be placed on eyeglasses for testing.

Hand movements (HM). A method of reporting vision that is insufficient for the reading of the Snellen chart and for the differentiation and counting of fingers, in which the examiner moves his or her hand at a relatively close distance to the eyes of the individual and records the distance, if any, at which movement is discernible.

Hemianopsia (hemianopia). Defective vision or blindness in half the visual field.

Hyperopia. A refractive error in which light rays from distant objects are brought to a focus behind the retina; farsightedness.

Individualized education program (IEP). A written plan of instruction for a child who receives special services, giving a statement of the student's present levels of educational performance, annual goals, short-term objectives, specific services needed by the student, dates when these services will begin and will be in effect, and related information. The plan is undertaken by a team including the child's parents. Under the Education for All Handicapped Children Act (P.L. 94-142), each student receiving special services must receive such a plan.

Intraocular. Inside the eye.

Iris. Colored, circular muscle suspended between the cornea and the lens of the eye. It separates the anterior and posterior chambers of the eye and is perforated in the center to form the pupil.

Jaeger test. A test for reading, in which lines of reading matter are printed in a series of type sizes that are often written as a series of letters and numbers (i.e., J#1, J#2, and so forth).

Keratoconus. A conical protrusion of the cornea associated with corneal thinning and scarring.

Keratometry. The measurement of corneal curvature.

Kinesthetic. Relating to tactile sensations and muscle movement in any part of the body.

Large print or type. Print that is larger than type commonly found in magazines, newspapers, and books. Ordinary print is usually 6 to 11 points in height (about 1/16 to 1/8 of an inch). Large type is 14 to 18 points in height (3/16 to 1/4 of an inch) or larger.

Laterality. A person's preference for using either the right or left side of the body and ability to interpret correctly the body's position with respect to right or left.

LEA. Local education agency.

Legally blind. Having central visual acuity of 20/200 or less in the better eye after best correction with conventional spectacle lenses, or visual acuity better than 20/200 if there is a field defect in which the widest diameter of the visual field is no greater than 20 degrees.

Lens. (1) A refractive medium. (2) The part of the eye that changes shape to adjust the focus of images from various distances into a sharp image on the retina (also called the *crystalline lens*).

Lentiglobus. An exaggerated curvature of the lens of the eye that produces a spherical bulging on the eye's anterior surface.

Light adaptation. The power of the eye to adjust itself to variations in the amount of light.

Light perception (LP). The ability to distinguish light from dark.

Light preference. Preference for a specific type of light or degree of illumination to accommodate a visual impairment, such as a preference for direct rather than indirect lighting or for dim rather than bright light.

Light projection. The ability to determine the direction of light.

Loupe. A small magnifier.

Low vision. Vision that can be used as a primary channel for learning (sometimes referred to as *partial sight*).

Low vision aids and devices. Optical devices of various types useful to persons with visual impairments. Magnifiers, monoculars, lenses, hand-held telescopes, and prism lenses are examples of low vision devices.

Low vision assessment. A comprehensive assessment of a visually impaired individual's visual impairment and visual potentialities and capabilities.

Low vision clinic. A clinic that gives eye examinations, provides low vision assessments, and prescribes low vision aids and devices and offers instruction on how to use them.

Macula. The small area of the retina that provides the most distinct vision.

Macular degeneration. A disease that affects cone cells in the macula and usually results in gradual loss of central vision but not in total blindness. It is often associated with aging.

Mobility. The ability to navigate from one's present position to one's desired position in another part of the environment. (See also **Orientation**.)

Monocular diplopia. A condition in which two images of the same object are seen by one eye.

Motor skills. Movement ability.

Multiply impaired. Having two or more concomitant disabilities that have a direct effect on learning ability.

Muscle balance. The ability of the six extraocular eye muscles of each eye to pull together to allow binocular vision to occur in all directions—vertically, horizontally, obliquely, and circularly.

Myopia. A refractive error in which the point of focus for rays of light from distant objects falls in front of the retina; nearsightedness.

Nearsightedness. Myopia.

Near vision. The ability to see objects distinctly at a comfortable reading distance.

Night blindness. A condition in which the rod function of the eye is diminished, causing deficient visual acuity at night and in dim light.

Nystagmus. A condition marked by involuntary, rapid movement of the eyeball. The movement may be lateral, vertical, rotary, or mixed.

Occipital cortex. The section of the brain that monitors visual sensations.

Ocular pursuit. The act of tracking a moving object in all directions—vertically, horizontally, obliquely, and circularly.

O.D. Oculus dexter; the right eye.

Ophthalmologist. A doctor of medicine (MD) who specializes in diagnosis and treatment of defects and diseases of the eye, performing surgery when necessary or prescribing other types of treatment, including eyeglasses or other optical devices.

Optic atrophy. Degeneration of the nerve tissue that carries messages from the retina to the brain.

Optician. A technician who, on prescription from a physician (ophthalmologist) or optometrist, grinds lenses, fits them into frames, fits contact lenses, and adjusts eyeglasses to the wearer.

Optic nerve. The group of nerve fibers that carry impulses from the retina to the brain.

Optometrist. A licensed, nonmedical specialist (OD) trained to work with the functioning but not the pathology of the eyes and who measures refraction and prescribes and fits eyeglasses.

Orientation. The process in which a blind or visually impaired person uses the remaining senses in establishing position and relationship to all other significant objects in the environment. (See also **Mobility**.)

Orientation and mobility (O&M). The field dealing with systematic techniques by which blind and visually impaired persons orient themselves to their environments and move about independently. See **Orientation; Mobility**.

Orthoptist. A nonmedical technician who directs and supervises ocular control training, or visual training involving the exercise of eye muscles to develop coordination and correct vision.

O.S. Oculus sinister; the left eye.

O.U. Oculi unitas; both eyes.

Paresis. Slight or partial paralysis.

Partially sighted. Having low vision.

Peripheral vision. The perception of objects, motion, or color by any part of the retina, excluding the macula.

Photophobia. Abnormal sensitivity to or discomfort from light.

Polycoria. The existence of more than one pupil in the eye.

Proprioceptive. Receiving stimulations within tissues of the body.

Ptosis. A paralytic drooping of the upper eyelid.

Pupil. The round opening in the center of the iris, which functions somewhat like the shutter opening of a camera. It permits light to enter the eye and appears as a black center in the iris.

Quadrantanopsia (quadrantanopia). Defective vision or blindness in one-fourth of the visual field.

Reading machine. A machine used to read printed material orally or tactilely.

Reading stand. A stand that supports regular or large-print books and allows the reader to change the position of the book.

Refraction. (1) The bending or deviation of rays of light in passing obliquely from one medium to another of different density. (2) The determination of the refractive errors of the eyes and their correction by the prescription of lenses.

Refractive error. A defect in the eye that prevents light rays from being brought to a single focus on the retina.

Residual vision. The useful sight remaining after a congenital defect, injury, illness, trauma, systemic disease, or ocular pathology has caused a vision loss.

Retina. The innermost coat of the eye, containing light-sensitive nerve cells and fibers connecting with the brain through the optic nerve.

Retinal detachment. A separation of the retina from the choroid.

Retinitis. Inflammation of the retina.

Retinitis pigmentosa (RP). Degeneration and atrophy of the light-sensitive rod cells of the retina.

Retinoblastoma. A tumor arising from the retinal germ cells. It is the most common malignant intraocular tumor of childhood, usually occurring before age 5.

Retinopathy of prematurity (ROP). See **Retrolental fibroplasia.**

Retinoschisis. A congenital cleft of the retina.

Retinoscopy. A method of objectively measuring refractive error by shining a light through the pupil and neutralizing its reflex with lenses.

Retrolental fibroplasia (RLF). A disease of the retina in which a mass of scar tissue fills the space between the back of the lens and the retina. Both eyes are affected in most cases. It occurs chiefly in infants born prematurely.

Rod. See **Cones and rods.**

Sclera. The white outer layer of the eye.

Scotoma (scotomata). A blind or partially blind area in the visual field.

SEA. State education agency.

Sensory stimulation. The process of rousing or invigorating the senses.

Shorelining. Orientation technique in which a blind or visually impaired person maintains physical contact with a surface, such as a building, other than the one on which he or she is walking.

Sighted guide techniques. Specific methods used by sighted people to guide blind or visually impaired people.

Sine correction (SC). Without correction; not wearing glasses.

Slate and stylus. Two tools used by hand to write in braille. A slate is a metal plate used to hold paper for hand brailling. A stylus is an instrument held in the hand and used to press braille dots on the paper held by the slate.

Snellen chart. A chart used for testing central visual acuity. It consists of lines of letters, numbers, or symbols in graded sizes drawn to specific measurements. Each size is labeled with the distance at which it can be read by the normal eye. It is most often used for testing vision at distances of 20 feet.

Stereoscopic vision (stereopsis). The ability to perceive the relative position of objects in space without such cues as shadows.

Strabismus. Failure of the two eyes to direct their gaze simultaneously at the same object because of muscle imbalance.

Suppression. Inattention to distracting or disturbing stimuli, often a forerunner of amblyopia.

Talking Book. An audio recording of a book, periodical, or other material. Talking Books are used in a federal program that provides equipment and recordings free on personal loan to blind or visually or physically disabled persons. Application is made through the Library of Congress National Library Service for the Blind and Physically Handicapped.

Talking calculator. Hand-held calculator that speaks each entry and result of calculations.

Telebinocular. Any stereoscopic instrument used for vision screening.

Tonometer. An instrument for measuring pressure inside the eye.

Tracking. The ability of the eye or eyes to follow an object systematically.

Trailing. Information-gathering and direction-taking techniques that are done using the hand or a cane.

Trauma. Injury, wound, or shock, or the resulting condition.

Tunnel vision. Contraction of the visual field to such an extent that only a small area of central visual acuity remains, giving the affected individual the impression of looking through a tunnel.

Visual acuity. Sharpness of vision with respect to the ability to discriminate detail.

Visual processing. The processing or use of the images acquired by the act of seeing.

Vitreous humor. The transparent, colorless mass of soft, jellylike material filling the space between the lens and the retina.

Vitreous turbidity. Cloudiness or haze in the vitreous humor.

WIRT Test. A test used for measuring stereoscopic vision.